THE WORKS OF SHAKESPEARE

EDITED FOR THE SYNDICS OF THE
CAMBRIDGE UNIVERSITY PRESS
BY
SIR ARTHUR QUILLER-COUCH
AND JOHN DOVER WILSON

THE TAMING OF THE SHREW

THE TAMING OF THE SHREW

CAMBRIDGE
AT THE UNIVERSITY PRESS
1968

PUBLISHED BY
THE SYNDICS OF THE CAMBRIDGE UNIVERSITY PRESS

Bentley House, 200 Euston Road, London, N.W. 1
American Branch: 32 East 57th Street, New York, N.Y. 10022

First Edition 1928
**Reprinted* 1953
1962
First Paperback Edition 1968

* Places where editorial changes or additions introduce variants from the first edition are, where possible, marked by a date [1952] in square brackets.

First printed in Great Britain at the University Press, Cambridge
Reprinted in Great Britain by Hazell Watson & Viney, Ltd., Aylesbury, Bucks

CONTENTS

THE TAMING OF THE SHREW

I

Coming to this comedy in our observance of the 1623 Folio's order, and in face of one of the most difficult cruxes in the Shakespearian Canon, we think it well to preface our approach to it with a brief but bold statement of the critical principles we have applied hitherto, and propose to apply, to questions of the authenticity, date, and so on of this or that play.

Our method has been accused as 'disintegrating' Shakespeare. We retort that no method at this time of day can, on condition of its being scholarly, do anything else, if we use the word intelligently. No one can pretend that Heminge and Condell's First Folio was a considered collection, revised by Shakespeare (after death) and bequeathed by him as his solemn claim on the worship of posterity. The First Folio has been proved—as might have been guessed from the twin names of its editors—to have been compiled from playhouse copies—piously, be it agreed, but not therefore with any exactness of research. It follows, then, that when we have an earlier Quarto of any given play, printed in the dramatist's lifetime—and not so far as we know disavowed by him—it has *prima facie* a good claim to be considered.

The consideration of these Quartos, and the claim of a number of them to give, quite often, a text more authentic than that of the First Folio, has been by all scholars admitted. The men, in fact, who have helped to substantiate this have done the greatest service to Shakespeare in their generation: and providing that they do not make—as they cannot and do not—any assertion of finality, we would urge that they at any rate work upon human probabilities. The old fashion was to assign any doubtful or inferior work of Shakespeare's to composition by several hands; and we are all familiar with 'Experts' who disagree in assigning this or that dozen lines of a given play to Marlowe, Dekker, Fletcher, Chapman. After some years of reading Shakespeare, testing our own inability and observing the talents of our fellows, we doubt if that confidence can be trusted, even in scholars of admitted learning.

But the difference resolves itself into two ways of 'disintegration.' The old way was to assume that Shakespeare, a man of supereminent genius, never fell below it, and that therefore, when the text exhibited rubbish or dirt, this rubbish was the contribution of a collaborator. (It would be interesting, could we discover it, to know all about the fellow who wrote all the worst lines in Shakespeare; almost as interesting as to discover something more about Shakespeare himself.) The new way is to suggest that the text of our author, as we have it, comes through playhouse copies and could (save by piracy) come through no other way. Which—men being what they are, and the stage and copyright being what they were—seems to our ignorance the more probable? Is it likelier that, for this or that play, Shakespeare should have sought through a library and worked with helpers, or that the Lord Chamberlain's Company should have trusted him to work *solus* upon any old play and then have altered it, here and there, to meet public taste? We know from Greene's famous attack upon him as a theatrical *factotum*, that Shakespeare did actually serve apprenticeship at this job and that his skill or success in it was not unnaturally resented by accredited playwrights with whose original compositions he made free: but even apart from this knowledge we ask bluntly 'Is it conceivable that any manager of a theatrical company, not being a fool and having discovered a young man who could do this sort of thing to admiration, would be at the cost of hiring a collaborator?' The supposition is as false to ordinary commercial prudence as it is to any experience of men who have had some acquaintance with the various ways in which masterpieces are written.

Moreover, and upon some acquaintance with Elizabethan writings, we may boldly challenge the pretence by any man—and the men who attempt have usually written no original work in their lives—to take a discussable play and parcel it up, assigning so many lines of it to Marlowe, so many to Massinger or to Fletcher, so many to authentic Shakespeare, so many of the rest to some wretched collaborator (happy in nothing but being innominate, unless happier belike in never having existed) who conveniently inserted whatsoever was flat, stale, unprofitable, bawdry, obscene, or by any twist of the idolatrous mind 'un-Shakespearian'; the truth being that Shakespeare could, in his large way, write bawdry, write flat passages (or at least let them pass in his process of refurbishing such and admit here and there spectacular effects artistically repugnant to him) such, for example, as the silly masque in *Cymbeline*.

In sum, while admitting that any true scholar reasonably conversant with his author can have the courage to say of almost any great passage that it is *aut* Shakespeare *aut nullus*, the pretension of anyone to assign such a remark as 'Muttons,' or 'I knew your father well,' or 'My lord, the carriage waits' from Shakespeare to somebody else on internal evidence postulates a priestly access to sources of information denied to simple men.

To assume as Shakespeare's a play advertised as Shakespeare's in the First Folio by Heminge and Condell (who knew him) is surely the sensible thing to do in absence of strong evidence of his having been helped by guessed-at collaborators of varying degrees of fame. To suggest that his text stands, as we have it, upon playhouse and prompt-book copies is as surely a simpler and more economical solution of a hundred difficulties. Nay, this and the whole business of 'piracy-publishing' and its methods—with the sort of authenticity that any cheap Quarto might claim—has been so carefully examined and elucidated for us by Dr A. W. Pollard and others as to leave the old pretensions of 'Experts' confidently assigning this line or that to this or that collaborator with Shakespeare—say Marlowe or Chapman—looking very foolish indeed. As it happens, we have in *The Taming of the Shrew*—in the play itself and in the story of its provenance—two cautionary illustrations of the dangers that lie in wait for the 'collaboration' theorist, to entrap him.

In the first place, our comedy in title and plot has an indisputable and close affinity with another (anonymous) one entitled *The Taming of A Shrew*: their histories in the publishing trade are entwined. This anonymous play contains not only sheaves of Marlowesque verse but a sheaf or two of Marlowe's actual writing, conveyed from *Tamburlaine* and *Faustus*: and yet (as we shall see) it is extremely doubtful that Marlowe had any conscious hand in it, or was responsible for it in any way.

Secondly, in dealing with our text of Shakespeare's play and working on the suggestion that a great deal of it is non-Shakespearian, we soon discover that either he wrote the whole of it or that we have to create for ourselves an innominate collaborator of such unusual talent that he is capable of being a poet, a skilled playwright or a complete fool indifferently and unexpectedly at any moment; in other words, that the good things occur in the midst of the bad, the bad in the midst of the good, and that to sift them out and assign them with confidence lays an intolerable strain upon self-sufficiency.

In 1857 Grant White, improving upon suggestions by Warburton and Steevens, evolved his theory of a collaborator who obligingly did the bad work and left Shakespeare to put in the good; and this theory has found wide acceptance ever since, though not by any means without disputants[1]. One of the most recent of these challengers, Dr Ernest P. Kuhl, has touched very neatly its fatal flaw.

The critics who follow the general conclusions of Grant White give to the unknown collaborator the underplot together with what they choose to call the 'poor touches' of the major part. To Shakespeare they assign the taming scenes, as well as some of the 'undoubtedly good touches' in the minor plot. This division at once confronts us with a curious problem by saddling this co-worker with an impossible task. He becomes a composite, hardly an individual. Strangely enough this difficulty seems to have escaped the observation of all save that shrewd critic Dr Furnivall. Though this venerable scholar believed that Shakespeare had an assistant, he declared that there was great danger of treating the play as if it were a plum-pudding, giving all the plums to Shakespeare (cf. *New Shakespear Soc.* 1874, 104). The truth of this statement becomes obvious when one recalls that the main source *The Taming of A Shrew* has plenty of plums. And conversely to mention but one Shakespearian play, *The Comedy of Errors*—accepted as genuine by all critics—abounds with glaring instances of 'poor touches.'

Collaboration in culinary art is not to be likened to collaboration in literary art. We are dealing not with a simple structure but with a piece of art; a play whose plot has been the admiration of generations; one of the best in Shakespeare[2].

To some small details in the above we might demur, but in general it well expresses the old fallacy of inventing an unknown collaborator to serve as whipping-boy for all Shakespeare's sins, real or supposed.

[1] Notably Miss Charlotte Porter, Mr J. M. Robertson, and Drs Gollancz and Boas.

[2] *Publications of the Modern Language Association of America*, vol. xi, no. 3 (reprinted 1925).

We know that Shakespeare could write sinfully as well as superbly—a defect, maybe, of his 'many-sidedness.' We can claim, perhaps on long familiarity with his writings and some acquaintance with the characteristic styles of other men, to give our opinion (yet always and only for what it is worth) on any disputed play or scene, saying pretty positively that it is or is not Shakespeare's. But the critic becomes exorbitant who professes himself able to take any play, dissect it almost line for line and distribute the portions to A or B or C, actual men or merely supposed: for that is more than our experience of human sagacity and human fallibility allows us to concede.

There lurks a further fallacy in the assumption that a writer of genius, touching up his work, always and consistently improves it as he revises. Who, for example, would claim this of Wordsworth, or of Burns? (Let anyone, for instance, compare the three versions of *The Banks o' Doon* and say if they show a consistency of improvement.) And if a poem may deteriorate under its author's own care, even more easily may a play, and yet again more easily might an Elizabethan play exposed from birth to the mercies of actors, promptmen and pirates—the moth and dust corrupting and the thieves breaking through to steal.

II

With the provenance of *The Shrew* our Note on the Copy deals in some detail. But we must prick out here some points of the outline.

(1) The text which every editor must use is that of the 1623 Folio. There was a later Quarto (1631), a careless reprint of this text, negligible by us for the moment. The later Folios have been collated with the First by Dr R. Warwick Bond (see his Introduction to

this play in *The Arden Shakespeare*) and we may take the word of so conscientious a scholar that the differences do not amount to much.

(2) Henslowe's *Diary* notes that a play *The Taming of a Shrew* was performed in June 1594 by the Lord Chamberlain's Servants (Shakespeare's Company) at Newington Butts. In their run of five or six nights they presented also *Titus Andronicus* and a *Hamlet*.

(3) In the previous May one Peter Short had entered at Stationers' Hall a play with the following title:

A Pleasant Conceited Historie, called The Taming of a Shrew, As it was sundry times acted by the Right honourable the Earle of Pembroke his servants. Printed at London by Peter Short and are to be sold by Cuthbert Burbie at his shop at the Royal Exchange, 1594. 7d.

This quarto, reprinted by Burby in 1596, conveyed by him to N. Ling in 1607, who published a third edition (used by Pope) in that year, and again transferred in the same year to John Smethwick who in 1631 substituted for our play the Quarto to which we have alluded, has hitherto been accepted most excusably as the play which Henslowe saw and the *verus fons* of our Comedy, which it resembles not only in title, general conception and main plot, but even in coincidences of quite good diction. Indeed, while every examination of the provenance must start from it, and always with difficulties enough, nothing at any rate seemed easier than to start by accepting it for an early version of *The Shrew* and working on that assumption—until Mr P. Alexander, the other day (*Times Literary Supplement*, Sept. 16, 1926), made the explosive suggestion that Short's quarto was not the play Henslowe saw, but a corrupt and degraded version, fudged by actors of Lord Pembroke's Company who, broken and out at heel, had sold that play to the Lord Chamberlain's Company but traded what they remembered of it to

Burby, and that Smethwick, to whom it had descended, in 1631 jettisoned it in favour of the right text of the 1623 Folio. For some other curious and intriguing questions conjured up by this version—henceforth distinguished here as *A Shrew* from Shakespeare's *The Shrew*—see VII. But we dismiss it for the moment to pass back to a yet earlier 'source' upon which Shakespeare's play largely, and the 1594 play pretty certainly though in far smaller measure, drew for the subsidiary plot of Bianca and her lovers.

(4) This is a comedy *I Suppositi*, written by Ariosto and produced by him with acclaim at Ferrara (his city) under patronage of the Duke's brother, the magnificently wicked Cardinal; transferred with more applause to Rome; re-cast later by its author into poor verse; and translated into English (prose) by George Gascoigne, who seems to have known the versified play while basing his work on the earlier one.

Gascoigne's title runs:

> *Supposes* a Comedie written in the Italian tongue by Ariosto Englished by George Gascoygne of Grayes Inne Esquire, and there presented 1566.

Here, on a sharp discovery that two such minds as Ariosto's and Shakespeare's once came within measurable distance of collaboration, if not of contact, we promise ourselves mighty sport. But the result is null, and mainly because Ariosto's Comedies, popular in their day, are null, by no means giving any measure of the man. They are ingenious after an accepted fashion; and Shakespeare borrowed the inventive tricks of *I Suppositi*. But, these used, Ariosto's play was emptied. It had none of the humorous and human stuff provided by the story of the Shrew and her tamer.

III

So we turn back from the intrigue of Ariosto to the real stuff of our play; the Induction and all the Petruchio-Katharina business. The 'sources' or 'derivation' of both of these can be dismissed by sensible men at once; the Induction theme—of the drunken sleeper awakened—being at least as old as the poem to the tale of Abu Hassan in *The Arabian Nights*, the shrew-taming scenes as old as the hills. Who ever possessed a grandfather that could not be roused from the chimney corner as by the sound of a trumpet to cap either of them with an analogous local tradition? The affair of the wives' wager at the end, too, is pure folk-lore. Shrews in especial, and stories of them, stick in the memories of old men who can 'mind' when there were such things as ducking-stools. And this kind of robust story imposed upon jejune Italian intrigue undoubtedly gives *The Shrew* a something racy, English and highly Elizabethan. *I Suppositi* has its polite revenge in civilising much of *A Shrew* which is in places coarse, and unforgivably coarse when it puts some of its grossest words into the mouth of Katharina. Indeed we may own not only of *A Shrew* but of *The Shrew* that they have not outworn the centuries comparably with the mass of Shakespeare's better plays. They are of primitive, somewhat brutal, stuff. We may not in this age have harked back to the chivalry of the Courts of Love or idealising of womanhood which the worship of Mary carried as a noble fashion into Court and tourney: we may understand as we read Chaucer the concomitance in his day of *Troilus* or *The Knight's Tale* with the lewder stories of his pilgrims, and even fit their meanings together intelligently in the *Prologue* and *Tale* of the *Wyfe of Bath*. But we do not and cannot, whether for better or worse, easily think of woman and her wedlock vow to obey quite in terms of—

> A spaniel, a wife and a walnut tree,—
> The more you whip 'em, the better they be.

Let us put it that to any modern civilised man, reading *A Shrew* or *The Shrew* in his library, the whole Petruchio business (in *A Shrew* he is called Ferrando) may seem, with its noise of whip-cracking, scoldings, its throwing about of cooked food, and its general playing of 'the Devil amongst the Tailors,' tiresome—and to any modern woman, not an antiquary, offensive as well. It is of its nature rough, *criard*: part of the fun of those fairs at which honest rustics won prizes by grinning through horse-collars.

IV

Nor can we at all agree with Johnson's pronouncement that 'of this play the two plots are so well united that they can hardly be called two without injury to the art with which they are interwoven.' In fact *The Shrew* abounds in 'loose ends' and sentences which assume in someone or other acquaintance with information not previously imparted (indicative of 'cuts' and patching); the hero, Petruchio, just drops in upon the intrigue from Verona without a why or wherefore and takes charge: anybody who meets anybody else in the street, no matter from what distance arrived, has always somehow known his father and his repute; while as for the back-chat of the serving-men, if not un-Shakespearian, it is frequently as silly-otiose as any we are tempted to redeem from Shakespeare in any play.

V

A Shrew and *The Shrew* are both prefaced by an 'Induction,' in which a drunkard on an ale-house bench in stupefied sleep, is discovered by a nobleman on his way from hunting, who plays a trick on him—just as the Caliph Haroun al-Raschid had played it on Abu Hassan—bidding his train carry the fellow home, dress him in fine raiment, and on his awaking conspire in solemn make-belief that he is a great lord come to his senses out of long insanity. In this framework, and for the victim's delectation, the main Comedy of intrigue is enacted. The shape of the Elizabethan stage and the seating of an Elizabethan theatre lent themselves to this kind of framework, and variations upon the device are not uncommon: the actor-spectators being either set apart or distributed among the real audience with licence to interrupt, 'gag' and comment.

It has become a tradition with critics to admire the Induction to *The Shrew*, to admire the whole business of Christopher Sly and the Master's improvement upon the framework of the 1594 play. To this, while agreeing in part, we in part demur. The Induction to *The Shrew* is quite good genuine Shakespeare and capitally managed up to a point; then the frame breaks up, dissolves, is lost. Sly fades straight out at the end of Act 1, Scene 1, and the rest of him is silence. Many excellent opportunities for clownish criticism (we may with proper modesty assert) are let go by. He ends on the admirable comment ''Tis a very excellent piece of work, madam lady: would 'twere done!' At this point, it may be urged, he might effectively and even spectacularly have gone off to sleep again and have snored at intervals during the long remainder of the Comedy. Well and convenient: but we do want to know what becomes of him at the end; and this little piece of satisfaction the Inductor of

1594 has provided for us. But who can he be, but Shakespeare? It was the 'manifestly better end' he provides, that made Pope, reluctantly, ascribe *A Shrew* to Shakespeare. He makes the lord's servants take the poor fellow and dispose him softly back on his ale-house bench again. Perhaps Shakespeare concluded upon an audible snore; or our demand has been a dull-witted one and the right ending was to close the curtain on silence. But, after all, it is not the way of authors to invite public attention so subtly to the dullness or insipidity of their own compositions. To vary a remark of the late and regretted A. B. Walkley, the scholars of Westminster annually turn their dormitory into a theatre, but the expert playwright does not intentionally return the compliment by turning his theatre into a dormitory.

Those of us who are old enough to remember *The Follies* and Pellissier's most successful device of distributing a part of his actors in upper boxes and stalls to 'guy' with profane interjections upon what happened on the stage itself, may think another suggestion worth considering: that Shakespeare, anticipating some such device, distributed his guyers in some similar way, and left the interjections to their own wit in improvising; such 'gag' never having been put on paper in the playhouse copy, would of course never reach the printer.

But this we allow to be merest conjecture.

In face of the many strange problems set by the concurrence and contrast of *A Shrew* and *The Shrew*, let us, almost in parenthesis, clear the decks of Ariosto and Gascoigne before discussing the two Inductions which open our way into the serious maze.

I Suppositi has no Induction. It undoubtedly supplied the sub-plot (not the 'taming' plot) of *The Shrew*, and possibly, but very far more faintly, parts of *A Shrew*. But with the real stuff of either it has little to do. The author of *Orlando Furioso*, though at pains to translate his prose version of *I Suppositi* into bald verse, cannot conceivably have taken pride in either (as no reader can derive satisfaction from the second, which is 'right butter-women's rank to market' on a nag of lengthened stride). He is even careless of his own city's geography. Reading Gascoigne, one is smitten in the eye by the old man Philogano's account of how he arrived from Sicily, *via* Ancona and Ravenna, at Ferrara, 'continually against the tide.' Says he—

> Honest man, it is even so: be you sure there is no love to be compared like the love of their parents towards their children. It is not long since I thought that a very weightie matter shoulde not have made me come out of *Sicilia*, and yet now I have taken this tedious toyle and travaile upon me, only to see my sonne, and to have him home with me.
>
> *Ferrarese*. By my faith, sir, it hath been a great travaile, indede too much for one of your age.
>
> *Philogano*. Yea be you sure. I came in companie with certaine gentlemen of my countrie, who had affaires to dispatche as far as to *Anticona*, from thence by water to *Ravenna*, and from *Ravenna* hither, *continually against the tide*.

But there in Ariosto it is (Act 4, Scene 3): save that Ariosto, knowing his country, says nothing about a 'tide.' With him it is simply *in contrario d'acqua*, or 'against the stream.' A careful treatise on the canal and river system of Italy in the sixteenth century (*a*) as it actually was, and (*b*) as it might be believed in by theatre-goers, has yet to be written.

VI

But we return to the Induction and, with that, to the beginning of serious business.

In our text of *The Shrew* we open upon a somnolent tinker on a bench outside an ale-house; upon whom happens a merry lord on the way home from hunting with pack and meinie. So it opens in *A Shrew*. But whereas in our play the merry lord talks as any merry lord naturally would—

> Huntsman, I charge thee, tender well my hounds...

in *A Shrew* he opens with—

> Now that the gloomie shaddow of the night
> Longing to view Orions drisling lookes
> Leapes from th'antarctic world unto the skies
> And dims the Welkin with his pitchie breath
> And darksome night oreshades the cristal heauens,
> Here break we off our hunting...

—an outburst that might well have set any retinue of huntsmen staring at one another. And so *A Shrew* plunges into passages not only Marlowesque, but sometimes lifted straight out of *Tamburlaine* or out of *Faustus*, word for word.

What shall be said of this, for example, when in *A Shrew* Ferrando (Petruchio) is courting Katarina?—

> Sweete Kate the[1] louelier then Dianas purple robe
> Whiter then are the snowie Apenis,
> Or icie haire that groes on Boreas chin.
> Father, I sweare by Ibis' golden beake,
> More faire and Radiente is my bonie Kate,
> Then siluer Zanthus when he doth imbrace,
> The ruddie Simies at Idas feete,
> And care not thou swete Kate how I be clad,
> Thou shalt haue garments wrought of Median silke,
> Enchast with pretious Iewells fetcht from far,
> By Italian Marchants that with Russian stemes,
> Plous vp huge forrowes in the Terren Maine,
> And better farre my louely Kate shall weare...[2]

What is this but the First Part of *Tamburlaine*, Act I, Scene 2?

[1] *Thou* Edd. 1596 and 1607.

[2] *A Shrew* in 'Shakespeare's Library' (Hazlitt's ed. Pt II, vol. ii, p. 513). Our references are to pages in this edition

> Zenocrate, lovelier than the love of Jove,
> Brighter than is the silver Rhodope,
> Fairer than whitest snow on Scythian hills...
> Thy garments shall be made of Median silk,
> Enchased with precious jewels....
>
> And Christian merchants that with Russian stems
> Plough up huge furrows in the Caspian sea,
> Shall sail to us, as lords of all the lake.

Dr Bond (with acknowledgments to Bullen and Courthope) has listed[1] some thirteen of these 'liftings' from *Tamburlaine* and *Faustus*, and to his list we may add *Tamburlaine*, Second Part, Act 4, Scene 3 init. (the famous 'jades of Asia' speech which, as it goes on, is clearly echoed in Ferrando's boasting that he will tame his bride's recalcitrance, come what may). Here are the passages:

Tamburlaine, Second Part, Act 4, Scene 3—

> The headstrong Iades of *Thrace*, *Alcides* tam'd
> That King *Egeus* fed with humaine flesh
> And made so wanton that they knew their strengths
> Were not subdew'd with valour more divine,
> Than you by this unconquered arme of mine.

A Shrew (p. 520)—

> *Fer.* Were she as stubborne or as full of strength
> As were the Thracian horse Alcides tamde,
> That King Egeus fed with flesh of men,
> Yet would I pull her down, and make her come
> As hungry hawkes do flie unto their lure.

VII

All these 'liftings' and echoings raise a number of questions and cross-questions which admit a wide speculation, but in the present stage of our ignorance (admitted ignorance being the parent of learning) may be briefly set out and left with a few comments.

[1] Introduction, p. xxxviii.

Question 1. Was the play *A Shrew* printed by Peter Short for Cuthbert Burby in 1594, 'as it was sundry times acted' by Pembroke's Servants, written by Marlowe, or by Marlowe in collaboration with others; and, if so, was Shakespeare one?

We know when and where and almost precisely how[1], Marlowe came to his end. He was slain with a dagger on the evening of May 30, 1593, in a room of entertainment at Deptford by one Ingram Frizer (or Frysar), an agent of Walsingham's, and in the presence of two notorious secret-service scoundrels, by name Nicholas Skeres and Robert Poley. There was no other witness. The three had spent the most of the day, walking up and down with Marlowe (himself an amateur in political intrigue), presumably trying to persuade him into saying or gainsaying something of which he held the secret. He was buried two days later, and Frizer after delay received a Pardon. Now it seems unlikely that anyone would have presented a year after this grim affair a play burlesquing Marlowe; most unlikely that our gentle Shakespeare—who on all evidence admired his 'dead Shepherd'—would have done so. It seems reasonable to give human decency the benefit of the doubt and suppose that *A Shrew*, though published in 1594, was presented, or at least written, before Marlowe's death in May 1593.

Question 2. But then, did Marlowe himself write it, with or without collaborators? To the more seriously minded this suggestion may appear incredible. But to those acquainted with stage-folk and their ways there is nothing incredible about it. Marlowe's was a mocking spirit; and one can, without any grave stretch of belief, imagine that after a thundering success with *Tamburlaine* he (and maybe some kindred spirits) would have exploited

[1] Thanks to the research of Mr J. Leslie Hotson: *The Death of Christopher Marlowe*. London: The Nonesuch Press, 1925.

its success by 'guying' his own bombast. As a theatrical, and commercial, hit the intrusion, upon a heathside pot-house, of a master of hounds who, to the amazement of his hunt, suddenly breaks into grandiose lines upon the 'Shadow of the Night longing to view Orion's drizzling looks,' might well have tickled ears that remembered them in high tragic setting.

Question 3. But if Marlowe had collaborators in this was Shakespeare one of them? To this we should have no hesitation in answering 'No,' were it not for just one touch which winds up Sly's interposition in the finale of *A Shrew*, which interposition, by the way, gets the comedy out of a bad *impasse*, and is in the right Warwickshire-Dogberry vein.

Question 4. Is it possible that the play which Henslowe saw acted at Newington Butts by the Lord Chamberlain's Servants in June 1594 was not *A Shrew* but actually Shakespeare's *The Shrew*, more or less as we have it?

The suggestion has much inherent probability, apart from the conjectural evidence brought by Mr Alexander to back it up (see II). And the suggestion amounts to this: that in or about 1592 the Earl of Pembroke's Company, having toured the provinces with *A Shrew*, etc. unsuccessfully, and returning to London hard-driven, disposed of their rights in this play to the Lord Chamberlain's Company (in which Shakespeare was then perhaps acting as general furbisher and *Johannes factotum*), and that out of *A Shrew* our young adapter of genius constructed *The Shrew* for his Company, piously cutting out the Marlowe, or most of it, and weaving in the plot of Ariosto-Gascoigne's *Supposes*[1]. If Shakespeare did this, and just so, we need not be worried that Meres does not include this play in his list in *Palladis Tamia*

[1] For a different interpretation of the facts, v. Note on the Copy, pp. 104–113.

(1598); for Shakespeare's job-work for his Company would, on any likelihood, have been done anonymously and even with some stealth.

This brings us to *Question* 5. If Shakespeare did this thing, as early as 1592, upon a play written by eminent hands and adapted it for a rival company, was *The Taming of the Shrew* by any chance the occasion of Greene's famous dying outburst, in the autumn of that year, denouncing the 'upstart crow beautified with our feathers', and not, as Sir Sidney Lee suggests, Shakespeare's patching upon *King Henry VI*[1]?

It will be seen that among these questions and along the alleys they open conjecture may wander at will and research in hope. We have merely indicated them, without pretence anywhere of a confident solution.

VIII

To call *The Shrew* a masterpiece is not only to bend criticism into sycophancy and a fawning upon Shakespeare's name. It does worse. Accepted, it sinks our standard of judgment, levels it, and by levelling forbids our understanding of how a great genius operates; how consummate it can be at its best, how flagrantly bad at its worst.

We hold that no-one walking on any such safe respectable level between heaven and hell can ever grasp the range of a Shakespeare to whom, in the writing of Comedy, *The Shrew* came in the day's work with (let us say) *Twelfth Night* or *The Tempest*. To pretend that *The Shrew*, with its 'prentice grasp on poetry, can compare for a moment with *A Midsummer-Night's Dream* or with *Twelfth Night* is an affectation, as foolish as most other human folly; as to assert *The Shrew's* underplot (the whole Ariosto intrigue) as

[1] *The Life of Shakespeare*, by Sir Sidney Lee, pp. 115–16.

master-work. Any careful, candid examination will expose it as patchwork, and patched none too cleverly.

But the trouble about *The Shrew* is that, although it reads rather ill in the library, it goes very well on the stage, in spite of the choice of managers and adapters to present it without the Induction—the one block of it which indelibly stamps it as Shakespeare's. Samuel Pepys on April 7, 1667, went to the King's house and

> there saw *The Taming of a Shrew* which hath some very good pieces in it, but generally is but a mean play; and the best part, 'Sawny' done by Tracy; and hath not half its life, by reason of the words, I suppose, not being understood at least by me.

Being a play which invites rant and in places even demands it, *The Shrew* as naturally tempts the impersonator of Petruchio to unintelligible shouting and mouthing. Yet there is a delicacy in the man underlying his boisterousness throughout, which should be made to appear, and, allowed to appear, is certain to please. He has to tame this termagant bride of his, and he does it in action with a very harsh severity. But while he storms and raves among servants and tailors, showing off for her benefit, to her his speech remains courteous and restrained—well restrained and, with its ironical excess, elaborately courteous. It is observable that, through all the trials he imposes on her, he never says the sort of misprising word that hurts a high-mettled woman more than any rough deed and is seldom if ever by any true woman forgotten or quite forgiven. This underlying delicacy observed by the actor presenting Petruchio, the play can never fail to 'act well,' or—as Pope and Johnson put it—to divert.

As for Katharina, only a very dull reader can miss recognising her, under her froward mask, as one of Shakespeare's women, marriageable and willing to mate; a Beatrice opposing a more repellent barrier, yet behind it willing, even seeking, to surrender. Her true quarrel with her sister Bianca (who has something in her of the pampered cat, with claws) slips out in the words which *A Shrew* gives to her—

> But yet I will consent and marry him;
> For I, methinks, have been too long a maid,
> And match him to [too], or else his manhood's good[1];

and in her outburst upon her father in *The Shrew*—

> *She* is your treasure, *she* must have a husband[2].

And there are truly few prettier conclusions in Shakespeare than her final submission—

> Nay, I will give thee a kiss, now pray thee, love, stay[3].

IX

There have been shrews since Xantippe's time and since Solomon found that a scolding woman was a scourge shaken to and fro: and it is not discreet perhaps for an editor to discuss, save historically, the effective ways of dealing with them. Petruchio's was undoubtedly drastic and has gone out of fashion. But avoiding the present times and recalling Dickens, most fertile of inventors since Shakespeare, with Dickens's long gallery of middle-aged wives who make household life intolerable by various and odious methods, one cannot help thinking a little wistfully that the Petruchian discipline had something to say for itself. It may be that these curses on the hearth are an inheritance of our middle-class, exacerbating wives by deserting them, most of the day, for desks and professional routine; that the high feudal lord would have none of it, and as little would the rough serf or labourer with an unrestrained hand. Let it suffice to say that *The Taming of the Shrew* belongs

[1] Sc. 5. 70–72. [2] Act 2, Sc. 1. [3] Act 5, Sc. 1.

to a period, and is not ungallant, even so. The works of our author do not enforce set lessons in morals. If we require moral instruction of them we must take them in the large and let the instruction almost imperceptibly sink in and permeate. He teaches no express doctrine anywhere, unless it be the value of charity as interpreting law. He is nowhere an expositor of creed or dogma, but simply always an exhorter, by quiet, catholic influence, to valiancy and noble conduct of life. Indeed it were no paradox to use even of this rough play the saying of St Jerome concerning the Son of Sirach, that we read Shakespeare not for establishment of doctrine but for improvement of manners.

[1928] Q.

TO THE READER

An obelisk (†) implies corruption or emendation and suggests a reference to the Notes.

A single bracket at the beginning of a speech signifies an 'aside.'

The reference number for the first line is given at the head of each page. Numerals in square brackets are placed at the beginning of the traditional acts and scenes.

Stage-directions quoted verbatim from the Folio are printed with inverted commas.

THE
TAMING OF THE SHREW

Scene: Padua, and Petruchio's house in the country

CHARACTERS IN THE PLAY

(a) The Induction

A Lord

CHRISTOPHER SLY, *a drunken tinker*

A Hostess

Page, Players, Huntsmen, and Servants attending on the Lord

(b) The Taming of the Shrew

BAPTISTA, *a rich gentleman of Padua*

VINCENTIO, *an old gentleman of Pisa*

LUCENTIO, *son to Vincentio, in love with Bianca*

PETRUCHIO, *a gentleman of Verona, suitor to Katharina*

GREMIO, HORTENSIO } *suitors to Bianca*

TRANIO, BIONDELLO, *a boy* } *servants to Lucentio*

GRUMIO, *a man of small stature, Petruchio's lackey*

CURTIS, *an aged serving-man, in charge of Petruchio's house in the country*

NATHANIEL, PHILIP, JOSEPH, NICHOLAS, PETER } *other servants to Petruchio*

A Pedant of Mantua

KATHARINA, *the Shrew*, BIANCA } *daughters to Baptista*

A Widow

Tailor, Haberdasher, and Servants attending on Baptista and Petruchio

THE TAMING OF THE SHREW

THE INDUCTION

[i.] *Before an alehouse on a heath*

The door opens and SLY *staggers out, driven forth by the Hostess*

Sly. I'll feeze you, in faith.

Hostess. A pair of stocks, you rogue!

Sly. Y'are a baggage, the Slys are no rogues....Look in the chronicles, we came in with Richard Conqueror... Therefore paucas pallabris, let the world slide: sessa!

Hostess. You will not pay for the glasses you have burst?

Sly. No, not a denier... Go by, S. Jeronimy—go to thy cold bed, and warm thee.

[*he totters forward and falls beneath a bush*

Hostess. I know my remedy, I must go fetch the third- 10 borough. [*she goes off*

Sly. Third, or fourth, or fifth borough, I'll answer him by law. I'll not budge an inch, boy: let him come, and kindly. ['*falls asleep*' *and begins to snore*

There is a sound of horns. A lord and his train are seen crossing the heath, as from hunting

Lord. Huntsman, I charge thee, tender well my hounds.
†Broach Merriman—the poor cur is embossed,
And couple Clowder with the deep-mouthed brach.
Saw'st thou not, boy, how Silver made it good

At the hedge corner, in the coldest fault?
20 I would not lose the dog for twenty pound.
1 *Huntsman.* Why, Belman is as good as he, my lord—
He cried upon it at the merest loss,
And twice to-day picked out the dullest scent.
Trust me, I take him for the better dog.
Lord. Thou art a fool. If Echo were as fleet,
I would esteem him worth a dozen such.
But sup them well, and look unto them all.
To-morrow I intend to hunt again.
1 *Huntsman.* I will, my lord. [*they see Sly*
30 *Lord.* What's here? one dead, or drunk? See, doth he breathe?
2 *Huntsman.* He breathes, my lord. Were he not warmed with ale,
This were a bed but cold to sleep so soundly.
Lord. O monstrous beast! how like a swine he lies!
Grim death, how foul and loathsome is thine image.
Sirs, I will practise on this drunken man.
What think you, if he were conveyed to bed,
Wrapped in sweet clothes, rings put upon his fingers,
A most delicious banquet by his bed,
And brave attendants near him when he wakes,
40 Would not the beggar then forget himself?
1 *Huntsman.* Believe me, lord, I think he cannot choose.
2 *Huntsman.* It would seem strange unto him when he waked.
Lord. Even as a flatt'ring dream or worthless fancy.
Then take him up, and manage well the jest:
Carry him gently to my fairest chamber,
And hang it round with all my wanton pictures:
Balm his foul head with warm distillèd waters,
And burn sweet wood to make the lodging sweet:

Procure me music ready when he wakes,
To make a dulcet and a heavenly sound; 50
And if he chance to speak, be ready straight
And with a low submissive reverence
Say 'What is it your honour will command?'
Let one attend him with a silver basin
Full of rose-water and bestrewed with flowers,
Another bear the ewer, the third a diaper,
And say 'Will't please your lordship cool your hands?'
Some one be ready with a costly suit,
And ask him what apparel he will wear;
Another tell him of his hounds and horse, 60
And that his lady mourns at his disease:
Persuade him that he hath been lunatic;
And when he says he is Sly, say that he dreams,
For he is nothing but a mighty lord.
This do, and do it kindly, gentle sirs—
It will be pastime passing excellent,
If it be husbanded with modesty.

1 *Huntsman.* My lord, I warrant you we will play our part,
As he shall think by our true diligence
He is no less than what we say he is. 70

Lord. Take him up gently and to bed with him,
And each one to his office when he wakes....
[*they bear Sly away. A trumpet sounds*
Sirrah, go see what trumpet 'tis that sounds—
[*a serving-man goes off*
Belike some noble gentleman that means,
Travelling some journey, to repose him here.

The serving-man returns

How now? who is it?

Serving-man. An't please your honour, players
That offer service to your lordship.
Lord. Bid them come near.

The players approach

Now, fellows, you are welcome.
Players. We thank your honour.
80 *Lord.* Do you intend to stay with me to-night?
A player. So please your lordship to accept our duty.
Lord. With all my heart. This fellow I remember,
Since once he played a farmer's eldest son—
'Twas where you wooed the gentlewoman so well:
I have forgot your name; but, sure, that part
Was aptly fitted and naturally performed.
A player. I think 'twas Soto that your honour means.
Lord. 'Tis very true—thou didst it excellent.
Well, you are come to me in happy time,
90 The rather for I have some sport in hand,
Wherein your cunning can assist me much.
There is a lord will hear you play to-night;
But I am doubtful of your modesties,
Lest over-eyeing of his odd behaviour—
For yet his honour never heard a play—
You break into some merry passion,
And so offend him: for I tell you, sirs,
If you should smile, he grows impatient.
A player. Fear not, my lord, we can contain ourselves,
100 Were he the veriest antic in the world.
Lord. Go, sirrah, take them to the buttery,
And give them friendly welcome every one—
Let them want nothing that my house affords.
[*a servant leads the players away*
Sirrah, go you to Barthol'mew my page,
And see him dressed in all suits like a lady:

That done, conduct him to the drunkard's chamber,
And call him 'madam,' do him obeisance:
Tell him from me, as he will win my love,
He bear himself with honourable action,
Such as he hath observed in noble ladies 110
Unto their lords, by them accomplishéd:
Such duty to the drunkard let him do,
With soft low tongue and lowly courtesy,
And say: 'What is't your honour will command,
Wherein your lady and your humble wife
May show her duty and make known her love?'
And then with kind embracements, tempting kisses,
And with declining head into his bosom,
Bid him shed tears, as being overjoyed
To see her noble lord restored to health, 120
Who for this seven years hath esteemed him
No better than a poor and loathsome beggar:
And if the boy have not a woman's gift
To rain a shower of commanded tears,
An onion will do well for such a shift,
Which in a napkin being close conveyed,
Shall in despite enforce a watery eye..
See this dispatched with all the haste thou canst—
Anon I'll give thee more instructions.

[*a servant departs*

I know the boy will well usurp the grace, 130
Voice, gait, and action of a gentlewoman:
I long to hear him call the drunkard husband,
And how my men will stay themselves from laughter
When they do homage to this simple peasant.
I'll in to counsel them: haply my presence
May well abate the over-merry spleen,
Which otherwise would grow into extremes.

[*he goes, the huntsmen following*

[ii.] *A richly furnished bedroom in the Lord's house*

SLY, clad in a night-dress, asleep in a chair with attendants at hand; 'some with apparel, others with basin and ewer and other appurtenances.' The Lord enters the room

Sly [*awakening*]. For God's sake, a pot of small ale.

1 *Servant.* Will't please your lordship drink a cup of sack?

2 *Servant.* Will't please your honour taste of these conserves?

3 *Servant.* What raiment will your honour wear to-day?

Sly. I am Christophero Sly, call not me 'honour' nor 'lordship': I ne'er drank sack in my life: and if you give me any conserves, give me conserves of beef: ne'er ask me what raiment I'll wear, for I have no more doublets than backs, no more stockings than legs, nor
10 no more shoes than feet, nay, sometime more feet than shoes, or such shoes as my toes look through the overleather.

Lord. Heaven cease this idle humour in your honour!
O, that a mighty man, of such descent,
Of such possessions and so high esteem,
Should be infuséd with so foul a spirit!

Sly. What, would you make me mad? Am not I Christopher Sly, old Sly's son of Burton-heath, by birth a pedlar, by education a card-maker, by transmutation
20 a bear-herd, and now by present profession a tinker? Ask Marian Hacket, the fat ale-wife of Wincot, if she know me not: if she say I am not xiiii. d. on the score for sheer ale, score me up for the lyingest knave in Christendom. [*a servant brings him a pot of ale*] What! I am not bestraught: here's— [*he drinks*

3 *Servant.* O, this it is that makes your lady mourn.

2 *Servant.* O, this it is that makes your servants droop.
Lord. Hence comes it that your kindred shuns
your house,
As beaten hence by your strange lunacy.
O, noble lord, bethink thee of thy birth, 30
Call home thy ancient thoughts from banishment,
And banish hence these abject lowly dreams:
Look, how thy servants do attend on thee,
Each in his office ready at thy beck.
Wilt thou have music? Hark! Apollo plays, ['*music*'
And twenty cagéd nightingales do sing.
Or wilt thou sleep? we'll have thee to a couch,
Softer and sweeter than the lustful bed
On purpose trimmed up for Semiramis.
Say thou wilt walk; we will bestrow the ground: 40
Or wilt thou ride? thy horses shall be trapped,
Their harness studded all with gold and pearl.
Dost thou love hawking? thou hast hawks will soar
Above the morning lark. Or wilt thou hunt?
Thy hounds shall make the welkin answer them,
And fetch shrill echoes from the hollow earth.
1 *Servant.* Say thou wilt course—thy greyhounds are
as swift
As breathéd stags: ay, fleeter than the roe.
2 *Servant.* Dost thou love pictures? we will fetch
thee straight
Adonis painted by a running brook, 50
And Cytherea all in sedges hid,
Which seem to move and wanton with her breath,
Even as the waving sedges play with wind.
Lord. We'll show thee Io as she was a maid,
And how she was beguiléd and surprised,
As lively painted as the deed was done.
3 *Servant.* Or Daphne roaming through a thorny wood,

Scratching her legs that one shall swear she bleeds,
And at that sight shall sad Apollo weep,
60 So workmanly the blood and tears are drawn.
Lord. Thou art a lord, and nothing but a lord:
Thou hast a lady far more beautiful
Than any woman in this waning age.
1 *Servant.* And till the tears that she hath shed for thee
Like envious floods o'er-run her lovely face,
She was the fairest creature in the world—
And yet she is inferior to none.
Sly. Am I a lord? and have I such a lady?
Or do I dream? or have I dreamed till now?
70 I do not sleep: I see, I hear, I speak;
I smell sweet savours and I feel soft things:
Upon my life, I am a lord indeed,
And not a tinker nor Christophero Sly.
Well, bring our lady hither to our sight—
And once again a pot o'th' smallest ale.
2 *Servant* [*presents the basin*]. Will't please your mightiness to wash your hands? [*Sly washes*
O, how we joy to see your wit restored!
O, that once more you knew but what you are!
These fifteen years you have been in a dream,
80 Or when you waked, so waked as if you slept.
Sly. These fifteen years! by my fay, a goodly nap.
But did I never speak of all that time?
1 *Servant.* O, yes, my lord, but very idle words,
For though you lay here in this goodly chamber,
Yet would you say ye were beaten out of door,
And rail upon the hostess of the house,
And say you would present her at the leet,
Because she brought stone jugs and no sealed quarts:
Sometimes, you would call out for Cicely Hacket.

Sly. Ay, the woman's maid of the house. 90

3 *Servant.* Why, sir, you know no house, nor no such maid,

Nor no such men as you have reckoned up,
As Stephen Sly, and old John Naps of Greece,
And Peter Turph, and Henry Pimpernell;
And twenty more such names and men as these,
Which never were nor no man ever saw.

Sly. Now, Lord be thankéd for my good amends!

All. Amen.

Sly. I thank thee, thou shalt not lose by it.

The page enters as a 'lady with attendants'; one proffers Sly a pot of ale

Page. How fares my noble lord? 100

Sly. Marry, I fare well—for here is cheer enough.
Where is my wife? [*he drinks*

Page. Here, noble lord, what is thy will with her?

Sly. Are you my wife and will not call me husband?
My men should call me 'lord,' I am your goodman.

Page. My husband and my lord, my lord and husband,
I am your wife in all obedience.

Sly. I know it well. What must I call her?

Lord. Madam.

Sly. Al'ce madam, or Joan madam? 110

Lord. 'Madam' and nothing else, so lords call ladies.

Sly. Madam wife, they say that I have dreamed
And slept above some fifteen year or more.

Page. Ay, and the time seems thirty unto me,
Being all this time abandoned from your bed.

Sly. 'Tis much! Servants, leave me and her alone.
[*the servants withdraw*
Madam, undress you and come now to bed.

Page. Thrice-noble lord, let me entreat of you

To pardon me yet for a night or two;
120 Or, if not so, until the sun be set:
For your physicians have expressly charged,
In peril to incur your former malady,
That I should yet absent me from your bed:
I hope this reason stands for my excuse.
Sly. Ay, it stands so that I may hardly tarry so long. But I would be loath to fall into my dreams again: I will therefore tarry in despite of the flesh and the blood.

1 *Servant re-enters*

1 *Servant.* Your honour's players, hearing your amendment,
Are come to play a pleasant comedy,
130 For so your doctors hold it very meet,
Seeing too much sadness hath congealed your blood,
And melancholy is the nurse of frenzy.
Therefore they thought it good you hear a play
And frame your mind to mirth and merriment,
Which bars a thousand harms and lengthens life.
Sly. Marry, I will; let them play it. Is not a †commodity a Christmas gambold or a tumbling-trick?
Page. No, my good lord, it is more pleasing stuff.
Sly. What, household stuff?
140 *Page.* It is a kind of history.
Sly. Well, we'll see't. Come, madam wife, sit by my side and let the world slip, we shall ne'er be younger.
[*the page sits beside him*

A 'flourish' of trumpets

THE TAMING OF THE SHREW

[1. 1.] *Padua. The houses of Baptista, Hortensio and others opening upon a public square; trees and a seat*

'LUCENTIO and his man TRANIO' enter the square

Lucentio. Tranio, since for the great desire I had
To see fair Padua, nursery of arts,
I am arrived for fruitful Lombardy,
The pleasant garden of great Italy,
And by my father's love and leave am armed
With his good will and thy good company,
My trusty servant, well approved in all,
Here let us breathe and haply institute
A course of learning and ingenious studies.
Pisa renownèd for grave citizens 10
Gave me my being and my father first,
A merchant of great traffic through the world,
Vincentio, come of the Bentivolii:
Vincentio's son, brought up in Florence,
It shall become to serve all hopes conceived.
To deck his fortune with his virtuous deeds:
And therefore, Tranio, for the time I study
Virtue, and that part of philosophy
Will I apply that treats of happiness
By virtue specially to be achieved. 20
Tell me thy mind, for I have Pisa left
And am to Padua come, as he that leaves
A shallow plash to plunge him in the deep,
And with satiety seeks to quench his thirst.
Tranio. Mi perdonato, gentle master mine:
I am in all affected as yourself,
Glad that you thus continue your resolve,

To suck the sweets of sweet philosophy.
Only, good master, while we do admire
30 This virtue and this moral discipline,
Let's be no stoics nor no stocks I pray,
Or so devote to Aristotle's checks,
As Ovid be an outcast quite abjured:
Balk logic with acquaintance that you have,
And practise rhetoric in your common talk,
Music and poesy use to quicken you,
The mathematics and the metaphysics
Fall to them as you find your stomach serves you:
No profit grows where is no pleasure ta'en...
40 In brief, sir, study what you most affect.
Lucentio. Gramercies, Tranio, well dost thou advise.
If, Biondello, thou wert come ashore,
We could at once put us in readiness,
And take a lodging fit to entertain
Such friends as time in Padua shall beget.
But stay awhile, what company is this?
Tranio. Master, some show to welcome us to town.

A door opens, and '*BAPTISTA, with his two daughters KATHARINA and BIANCA,*' *followed by* '*GREMIO, a pantaloon,*' *and* '*HORTENSIO, suitor to Bianca,*' *come out.* '*Lucentio and Tranio stand by*' *among the trees*

Baptista. Gentlemen, importune me no farther,
For how I firmly am resolved you know;
50 That is, not to bestow my youngest daughter,
Before I have a husband for the elder:
If either of you both love Katharina,
Because I know you well, and love you well,
Leave shall you have to court her at your pleasure.
Gremio. To cart her rather: she's too rough for me.
There, there, Hortensio, will you any wife?

Katharina. I pray you, sir, is it your will
To make a stale of me amongst these mates?
Hortensio. Mates, maid! how mean you that? no mates for you,
Unless you were of gentler, milder mould. 60
Katharina. I'faith, sir, you shall never need to fear.
Iwis it is not half way to her heart:
But if it were, doubt not her care should be
To comb your noddle with a three-legged stool,
And paint your face, and use you like a fool.
Hortensio. From all such devils, good Lord deliver us!
Gremio. And me too, good Lord!
(*Tranio.* Husht, master! here's some good pastime toward;
That wench is stark mad or wonderful froward.
(*Lucentio.* But in the other's silence do I see 70
Maid's mild behaviour and sobriety.
Peace, Tranio.
(*Tranio.* Well said, master—mum! and gaze your fill.
Baptista. Gentlemen, that I may soon make good
What I have said, Bianca, get you in.
And let it not displease thee, good Bianca,
For I will love thee ne'er the less, my girl.
[*he fondles her*
Katharina. A pretty peat! it is best
Put finger in the eye, an she knew why.
Bianca. Sister, content you in my discontent. 80
Sir, to your pleasure humbly I subscribe:
My books and instruments shall be my company,
On them to look and practise by myself.
(*Lucentio.* Hark, Tranio! thou mayst hear Minerva speak.

Hortensio. Signior Baptista, will you be so strange?
Sorry am I that our good will effects
Bianca's grief.
Gremio. Why will you mew her up,
Signior Baptista, for this fiend of hell,
And make her bear the penance of her tongue?
90 *Baptista.* Gentlemen, content ye; I am resolved:
Go in, Bianca.... [*Bianca goes in*
And for I know she taketh most delight
In music, instruments and poetry,
Schoolmasters will I keep within my house,
Fit to instruct her youth. If you, Hortensio,
Or Signior Gremio, you, know any such,
Prefer them hither; for to cunning men
I will be very kind, and liberal
To mine own children in good bringing-up.
100 And so farewell...Katharina you may stay,
For I have more to commune with Bianca. [*he goes in*
Katharina. Why, and I trust I may go too, may I not?
What, shall I be appointed hours, as though, belike,
I knew not what to take, and what to leave? Ha!
[*she turns upon her heel*
Gremio. You may go to the devil's dam: your gifts are so good, here's none will hold you. [*she enters the house and claps to the door behind her*] There! love is not so great, Hortensio, but we may blow our nails together, and fast it fairly out: our cake's dough on both sides.
110 Farewell: yet, for the love I bear my sweet Bianca, if I can by any means light on a fit man to teach her that wherein she delights, I will wish him to her father.
Hortensio. So will I, Signior Gremio: but a word, I pray. Though the nature of our quarrel yet never brooked parle, know now, upon advice, it toucheth us both—that we may yet again have access to our fair

mistress and be happy rivals in Bianca's love—to labour and effect one thing specially.

Gremio. What's that, I pray?

Hortensio. Marry, sir, to get a husband for her sister. 120

Gremio. A husband! a devil.

Hortensio. I say, a husband.

Gremio. I say, a devil. Think'st thou, Hortensio, though her father be very rich, any man is so very a fool to be married to hell?

Hortensio. Tush, Gremio: though it pass your patience and mine to endure her loud alarums, why, man, there be good fellows in the world, an a man could light on them, would take her with all faults, and money enough.

Gremio. I cannot tell: but I had as lief take her dowry 130 with this condition—to be whipped at the high-cross every morning.

Hortensio. Faith, as you say, there's small choice in rotten apples. But come, since this bar in law makes us friends, it shall be so far forth friendly maintained till by helping Baptista's eldest daughter to a husband we set his youngest free for a husband, and then have to't afresh. Sweet Bianca! Happy man be his dole! He that runs fastest gets the ring. How say you, Signior Gremio? 140

Gremio. I am agreed, and would I had given him the best horse in Padua to begin his wooing that would thoroughly woo her, wed her and bed her and rid the house of her! Come on. [*they go off together*

Tranio. I pray, sir, tell me, is it possible
That love should of a sudden take such hold?

Lucentio. O Tranio, till I found it to be true,
I never thought it possible or likely;
But see, while idly I stood looking on,
I found the effect of love in idleness, 150

And now in plainness do confess to thee—
That art to me as secret and as dear
As Anna to the Queen of Carthage was—
Tranio, I burn, I pine, I perish, Tranio,
If I achieve not this young modest girl.
Counsel me, Tranio, for I know thou canst:
Assist me, Tranio, for I know thou wilt.
Tranio. Master, it is no time to chide you now;
Affection is not rated from the heart:
160 If love have touched you, nought remains but so—
'Redime te captum quam queas minimo.'
Lucentio. Gramercies, lad. Go forward, this contents.
The rest will comfort, for thy counsel's sound.
Tranio. Master, you looked so longly on the maid,
Perhaps you marked not what's the pith of all.
Lucentio. O yes, I saw sweet beauty in her face,
Such as the daughter of Agenor had,
That made great Jove to humble him to her hand,
When with his knees he kissed the Cretan strand.
170 *Tranio.* Saw you no more? marked you not how her sister
Began to scold and raise up such a storm
That mortal ears might hardly endure the din?
Lucentio. Tranio, I saw her coral lips to move,
And with her breath she did perfume the air.
Sacred and sweet was all I saw in her.
Tranio. Nay, then 'tis time to stir him from his trance.
I pray, awake, sir: if you love the maid,
Bend thoughts and wits to achieve her. Thus it stands:
Her elder sister is so curst and shrewd
180 That till the father rid his hands of her,
Master, your love must live a maid at home,
And therefore has he closely mewed her up,
Because he will not be annoyed with suitors.

Lucentio. Ah, Tranio, what a cruel father's he!
But art thou not advised, he took some care
To get her cunning schoolmasters to instruct her?
Tranio. Ay, marry, am I, sir—and now 'tis plotted.
Lucentio. I have it, Tranio.
Tranio. Master, for my hand,
Both our inventions meet and jump in one!
Lucentio. Tell me thine first.
Tranio. You will be schoolmaster, 190
And undertake the teaching of the maid:
That's your device.
Lucentio. It is: may it be done?
Tranio. Not possible; for who shall bear your part,
And be in Padua here Vincentio's son,
Keep house and ply his book, welcome his friends,
Visit his countrymen and banquet them?
Lucentio. Basta, content thee; for I have it full.
We have not yet been seen in any house,
Nor can we be distinguished by our faces
For man or master: then it follows thus; 200
Thou shalt be master, Tranio, in my stead,
Keep house and port and servants, as I should:
I will some other be—some Florentine,
Some Neapolitan, or mean man of Pisa.
'Tis hatched, and shall be so: Tranio, at once
Uncase thee; take my coloured hat and cloak:
When Biondello comes, he waits on thee,
But I will charm him first to keep his tongue.
Tranio. So had you need. [*they change habits*
In brief, sir, sith it your pleasure is, 210
And I am tied to be obedient—
For so your father charged me at our parting;
'Be serviceable to my son,' quoth he,
Although I think 'twas in another sense—

I am content to be Lucentio,
Because so well I love Lucentio.
Lucentio. Tranio, be so, because Lucentio loves,
And let me be a slave, t'achieve that maid
Whose sudden sight hath thralled my wounded eye.

BIONDELLO approaches

220 Here comes the rogue. Sirrah, where have you been?
Biondello. Where have I been! Nay, how now! where are you?
Master, has my fellow Tranio stol'n your clothes?
Or you stol'n his? or both? pray, what's the news?
Lucentio. Sirrah, come hither. 'Tis no time to jest,
And therefore frame your manners to the time.
Your fellow Tranio here, to save my life,
Puts my apparel and my count'nance on,
And I for my escape have put on his;
For in a quarrel since I came ashore
230 I killed a man and fear I was descried:
Wait you on him, I charge you, as becomes,
While I make way from hence to save my life:
You understand me?
Biondello. Ay, sir, ne'er a whit.
Lucentio. And not a jot of Tranio in your mouth.
Tranio is changed into Lucentio.
Biondello. The better for him, would I were so too!
Tranio. So could I, faith, boy, to have the next wish after,
That Lucentio indeed had Baptista's youngest daughter.
But, sirrah, not for my sake, but your master's, I advise
240 You use your manners discreetly in all kind of companies:
When I am alone, why, then I am Tranio;
But in all places else, your master Lucentio.

Lucentio. Tranio, let's go:
One thing more rests, that thyself execute,
To make one among these wooers: if thou ask me why,
Sufficeth my reasons are both good and weighty.

[*they go*

'*The presenters above speak*'

1 *Servant.* My lord, you nod, you do not mind the play.
Sly [*awakes*]. Yes, by Saint Anne, do I. A good matter, surely: comes there any more of it?
Page. My lord, 'tis but begun. 250
Sly. 'Tis a very excellent piece of work, madam lady: would 'twere done! ['*they sit and mark*'

[1. 2.] *Padua; the square, as before*

'*PETRUCHIO and his man GRUMIO*' *draw near Hortensio's house*

Petruchio. Verona, for a while I take my leave,
To see my friends in Padua, but of all
My best belovéd and approvéd friend,
Hortensio; and I trow this is his house...
Here, sirrah Grumio, knock, I say.
Grumio. Knock, sir! whom should I knock? is there any man has rebused your worship?
Petruchio. Villain, I say, knock me here soundly.
Grumio. Knock you here, sir? why, sir, what am I, sir, that I should knock you here, sir? 10
Petruchio. Villain, I say, knock me at this gate,
And rap me well, or I'll knock your knave's pate.
Grumio. My master is grown quarrelsome: I should knock you first,
And then I know after who comes by the worst.
Petruchio. Will it not be?

Faith, sirrah, an you'll not knock, I'll ring it!
I'll try how you can 'sol, fa,' and sing it.
['*he wrings him by the ears*'

Grumio. Help, masters, help! my master is mad.
Petruchio. Now, knock when I bid you: sirrah! villain!

HORTENSIO opens

20 *Hortensio.* How now! what's the matter? My old friend Grumio! and my good friend Petruchio! How do you all at Verona?

Petruchio. Signior Hortensio, come you to part the fray?
'Con tutto il cuore, ben trovato,' may I say.

Hortensio. 'Alla nostra casa ben venuto, molto honorato signor mio Petruchio.'
Rise, Grumio, rise, we will compound this quarrel.

Grumio. Nay, 'tis no matter, sir, what he 'leges in Latin. If this be not a lawful cause for me to leave his 30 service, look you, sir. He bid me knock him and rap him soundly, sir: well, was it fit for a servant to use his master so, being perhaps (for aught I see) two and thirty, a pip out?
Whom would to God I had well knocked at first,
Then had not Grumio come by the worst.

Petruchio. A senseless villain! Good Hortensio,
I bade the rascal knock upon your gate,
And could not get him for my heart to do it.

Grumio. Knock at the gate! O heavens! Spake you 40 not these words plain, 'Sirrah, knock me here: rap me here: knock me well, and knock me soundly'? And come you now with 'knocking at the gate'?

Petruchio. Sirrah, be gone, or talk not, I advise you.
Hortensio. Petruchio, patience, I am Grumio's pledge:

Why, this' a heavy chance 'twixt him and you,
Your ancient, trusty, pleasant servant Grumio.
And tell me now, sweet friend, what happy gale
Blows you to Padua here from old Verona?

Petruchio. Such wind as scatters young men through the world,
To seek their fortunes farther than at home, 50
Where small experience grows but in a few.
Signior Hortensio, thus it stands with me—
Antonio, my father, is deceased,
And I have thrust myself into this maze,
Haply to wive and thrive as best I may:
Crowns in my purse I have, and goods at home,
And so am come abroad to see the world.

Hortensio. Petruchio, shall I then come roundly to thee,
And wish thee to a shrewd ill-favoured wife?
Thou'dst thank me but a little for my counsel: 60
And yet I'll promise thee she shall be rich,
And very rich: but th'art too much my friend,
And I'll not wish thee to her.

Petruchio. Signior Hortensio, 'twixt such friends as we,
Few words suffice: and therefore, if thou know
One rich enough to be Petruchio's wife—
As wealth is burden of my wooing dance—
Be she as foul as was Florentius' love,
As old as Sibyl, and as curst and shrewd
As Socrates' Xanthippe, or a worse, 70
She moves me not, or not removes, at least,
Affection's edge in me, were she as rough
As are the swelling Adriatic seas.
I come to wive it wealthily in Padua;
If wealthily, then happily in Padua.

Grumio. Nay, look you, sir, he tells you flatly what his mind is: why, give him gold enough, and marry him

to a puppet or an aglet-baby, or an old trot with ne'er a tooth in her head, though she have as many diseases
80 as two and fifty horses: why, nothing comes amiss, so money comes withal.

Hortensio. Petruchio, since we are stepped thus far in,
I will continue that I broached in jest.
I can, Petruchio, help thee to a wife
With wealth enough, and young and beauteous,
Brought up as best becomes a gentlewoman.
Her only fault, and that is faults enough,
Is that she is intolerable curst
And shrewd and froward, so beyond all measure,
90 That, were my state far worser than it is,
I would not wed her for a mine of gold.

Petruchio. Hortensio, peace; thou know'st not gold's effect.
Tell me her father's name and 'tis enough;
For I will board her, though she chide as loud
As thunder when the clouds in autumn crack.

Hortensio. Her father is Baptista Minola,
An affable and courteous gentleman,
Her name is Katharina Minola,
Renowned in Padua for her scolding tongue.

100 *Petruchio.* I know her father, though I know not her,
And he knew my deceaséd father well:
I will not sleep, Hortensio, till I see her,
And therefore let me be thus bold with you,
To give you over at this first encounter,
Unless you will accompany me thither.

Grumio. I pray you, sir, let him go while the humour lasts. O' my word, an she knew him as well as I do, she would think scolding would do little good upon him. She may perhaps call him half a score knaves or
110 so: why, that's nothing; an he begin once, he'll rail in

his rope-tricks. I'll tell you what, sir, an she stand him but a little, he will throw a figure in her face, and so disfigure her with it, that she shall have no more eyes to see withal than a cat. You know him not, sir.

Hortensio. Tarry, Petruchio, I must go with thee,
For in Baptista's keep my treasure is:
He hath the jewel of my life in hold,
His youngest daughter, beautiful Bianca,
And her withholds from me and other more,
Suitors to her and rivals in my love; 120
Supposing it a thing impossible,
For those defects I have before rehearsed,
That ever Katharina will be wooed:
Therefore this order hath Baptista ta'en,
That none shall have access unto Bianca,
Till Katharine the curst have got a husband.

Grumio. Katharine the curst!
A title for a maid of all titles the worst.

Hortensio. Now shall my friend Petruchio do
me grace,
And offer me disguised in sober robes 130
To old Baptista as a schoolmaster
Well seen in music, to instruct Bianca,
That so I may by this device at least
Have leave and leisure to make love to her,
And unsuspected court her by herself.

Grumio. Here's no knavery! See, to beguile the old folks, how the young folks lay their heads together!

GREMIO enters the square, with 'LUCENTIO disguised' as Cambio, a schoolmaster

Master, master, look about you: who goes there? ha!

Hortensio. Peace, Grumio! it is the rival of my love.
Petruchio, stand by a while. 140

(*Grumio.* A proper stripling and an amorous!
[*they stand by*

Gremio. O, very well—I have perused the note.
Hark you, sir, I'll have them very fairly bound—
All books of love, see that at any hand—
And see you read no other lectures to her:
You understand me. Over and beside
Signior Baptista's liberality,
I'll mend it with a largess. [*returning the note*] Take your paper too.
And let me have them very well perfumed;
150 For she is sweeter than perfume itself,
To whom they go. What will you read to her?

Lucentio. Whate'er I read to her, I'll plead for you
As for my patron, stand you so assured,
As firmly as yourself were still in place,
Yea, and perhaps with more successful words
Than you, unless you were a scholar, sir.

Gremio. O this learning, what a thing it is!

(*Grumio.* O this woodcock, what an ass it is!

(*Petruchio.* Peace, sirrah.

160 (*Hortensio.* Grumio, mum!
[*comes forward*] God save you, Signior Gremio!

Gremio. And you are well met, Signior Hortensio.
Trow you whither I am going? To Baptista Minola.
I promised to inquire carefully
About a schoolmaster for the fair Bianca,
And by good fortune I have lighted well
On this young man; for learning and behaviour
Fit for her turn, well read in poetry
And other books—good ones, I warrant ye.

Hortensio. 'Tis well: and I have met a gentleman
170 Hath promised me to help me to another,
A fine musician to instruct our mistress,

So shall I no whit be behind in duty
To fair Bianca, so beloved of me.
Gremio. Beloved of me, and that my deeds shall prove.
(*Grumio.* And that his bags shall prove.
Hortensio. Gremio, 'tis now no time to vent our love.
Listen to me, and if you speak me fair,
I'll tell you news indifferent good for either.
Here is a gentleman whom by chance I met,
Upon agreement from us to his liking, 180
Will undertake to woo curst Katharine,
Yea, and to marry her, if her dowry please.
Gremio. So said, so done, is well.
Hortensio, have you told him all her faults?
Petruchio. I know she is an irksome brawling scold:
If that be all, masters, I hear no harm.
Gremio. No, say'st me so, friend? What countryman?
Petruchio. Born in Verona, old Antonio's son:
My father dead, my fortune lives for me,
And I do hope good days and long to see. 190
Gremio. Sir, such a life, with such a wife, were strange!
But, if you have a stomach, to't a God's name—
You shall have me assisting you in all.
But will you woo this wild-cat?
Petruchio. Will I live?
Grumio. Will he woo her? ay, or I'll hang her.
Petruchio. Why came I hither but to that intent?
Think you a little din can daunt mine ears?
Have I not in my time heard lions roar?
Have I not heard the sea puffed up with winds
Rage like an angry boar chaféd with sweat? 200
Have I not heard great ordnance in the field,
And heaven's artillery thunder in the skies?
Have I not in a pitchéd battle heard

Loud 'larums, neighing steeds, and trumpets' clang?
And do you tell me of a woman's tongue,
That gives not half so great a blow to hear,
As will a chestnut in a farmer's fire?
Tush! tush! fear boys with bugs.

Grumio. For he fears none.

Gremio. Hortensio, hark:

210 This gentleman is happily arrived,
My mind presumes, for his own good and ours.

Hortensio. I promised we would be contributors
And bear his charge of wooing, whatsoe'er.

Gremio. And so we will, provided that he win her.

Grumio. I would I were as sure of a good dinner.

TRANIO, bravely apparelled as Lucentio, swaggers up with BIONDELLO

Tranio. Gentlemen, God save you! If I may be bold,
Tell me, I beseech you, which is the readiest way
To the house of Signior Baptista Minola?

Biondello. He that has the two fair daughters: is't he you mean?

220 *Tranio.* Even he, Biondello.

Gremio. Hark you, sir! You mean not her too?

Tranio. Perhaps, him and her, sir. What have you to do?

Petruchio. Not her that chides, sir, at any hand, I pray.

Tranio. I love no chiders, sir: Biondello, let's away.

(*Lucentio.* Well begun, Tranio.

Hortensio. Sir, a word ere you go:
Are you a suitor to the maid you talk of, yea or no?

Tranio. And if I be, sir, is it any offence?

Gremio. No; if without more words you will get you hence.

Tranio. Why, sir, I pray, are not the streets as free
For me as for you?
Gremio. But so is not she. 230
Tranio. For what reason, I beseech you?
Gremio. For this reason, if you'll know,
That she's the choice love of Signior Gremio.
Hortensio. That she's the chosen of Signior Hortensio.
Tranio. Softly, my masters! if you be gentlemen,
Do me this right; hear me with patience.
Baptista is a noble gentleman,
To whom my father is not all unknown,
And were his daughter fairer than she is,
She may more suitors have and me for one.
Fair Leda's daughter had a thousand wooers, 240
Then well one more may fair Bianca have:
And so she shall; Lucentio shall make one,
Though Paris came in hope to speed alone.
Gremio. What, this gentleman will out-talk us all!
Lucentio. Sir, give him head, I know he'll prove a jade.
Petruchio. Hortensio, to what end are all these words?
Hortensio. Sir, let me be so bold as ask you,
Did you yet ever see Baptista's daughter?
Tranio. No, sir, but hear I do that he hath two:
The one as famous for a scolding tongue, 250
As is the other for beauteous modesty.
Petruchio. Sir, sir, the first's for me, let her go by.
Gremio. Yea, leave that labour to great Hercules,
And let it be more than Alcides' twelve.
Petruchio. Sir, understand you this of me in sooth,
The youngest daughter whom you hearken for
Her father keeps from all access of suitors,
And will not promise her to any man,
Until the elder sister first be wed.
The younger then is free, and not before. 260

Tranio. If it be so, sir, that you are the man
Must stead us all and me amongst the rest;
And if you break the ice and do this feat,
Achieve the elder, set the younger free
For our access—whose hap shall be to have her
Will not so graceless be to be ingrate.
Hortensio. Sir, you say well, and well you do conceive,
And since you do profess to be a suitor,
You must, as we do, gratify this gentleman,
270 To whom we all rest generally beholding.
Tranio. Sir, I shall not be slack, in sign whereof,
Please ye we may contrive this afternoon,
And quaff carouses to our mistress' health,
And do as adversaries do in law,
Strive mightily, but eat and drink as friends.
Grumio, Biondello. O excellent motion! Fellows, let's be gone.
Hortensio. The motion's good indeed, and be it so,
Petruchio, I shall be your ben venuto. [*they go*

[2. 1.] *A room in the house of Baptista*

KATHARINA with a whip stands over BIANCA, who crouches by the wall, her hands tied behind her

Bianca. Good sister, wrong me not, nor wrong yourself,
To make a bondmaid and a slave of me.
That I disdain: but for these other gauds,
Unbind my hands, I'll pull them off myself,
Yea, all my raiment, to my petticoat,
Or what you will command me will I do,
So well I know my duty to my elders.
Katharina. Of all thy suitors, here I charge thee, tell
Whom thou lov'st best: see thou dissemble not.
10 *Bianca.* Believe me, sister, of all the men alive

I never yet beheld that special face
Which I could fancy more than any other.
Katharina. Minion, thou liest: is't not Hortensio?
Bianca. If you affect him, sister, here I swear
I'll plead for you myself, but you shall have him.
Katharina. O then, belike, you fancy riches more—
You will have Gremio to keep you fair.
Bianca. Is it for him you do envy me so?
Nay then you jest, and now I well perceive
You have but jested with me all this while: 20
I prithee, sister Kate, untie my hands.
Katharina [*'strikes her'*]. If that be jest, then all the rest was so.

BAPTISTA enters

Baptista. Why, how now, dame! whence grows this insolence?
Bianca, stand aside. Poor girl! she weeps.
[*he unbinds her hands*
Go ply thy needle, meddle not with her.
For shame, thou hilding of a devilish spirit,
Why dost thou wrong her that did ne'er wrong thee?
When did she cross thee with a bitter word?
Katharina. Her silence flouts me, and I'll be revenged.
[*'flies after Bianca'*
Baptista [*checks her*]. What, in my sight? Bianca, get thee in. [*Bianca departs* 30
Katharina. What, will you not suffer me? Nay, now I see
She is your treasure, she must have a husband,
I must dance bare-foot on her wedding-day
And for your love to her lead apes in hell.
Talk not to me, I will go sit and weep
Till I can find occasion of revenge. [*she flings out*

Baptista. Was ever gentleman thus grieved as I?
But who comes here?

GREMIO enters, with LUCENTIO as Cambio the schoolmaster, PETRUCHIO, with HORTENSIO as Licio the musician, and TRANIO as Lucentio, 'with his boy bearing a lute and books'

Gremio. Good morrow, neighbour Baptista.
40 *Baptista.* Good morrow, neighbour Gremio. [*he bows*] God save you, gentlemen!
Petruchio. And you, good sir: pray, have you not a daughter
Called Katharina, fair and virtuous?
Baptista. I have a daughter, sir, called Katharina.
Gremio. You are too blunt, go to it orderly.
Petruchio. You wrong me, Signior Gremio, give me leave.
I am a gentleman of Verona, sir,
That, hearing of her beauty and her wit,
Her affability and bashful modesty.
[*Baptista throws up his hands*
50 Her wondrous qualities, and mild behaviour,
Am bold to show myself a forward guest
Within your house, to make mine eye the witness
Of that report which I so oft have heard.
And, for an entrance to my entertainment,
I do present you with a man of mine,
[*presenting Hortensio*
Cunning in music and the mathematics,
To instruct her fully in those sciences,
Whereof I know she is not ignorant.
Accept of him, or else you do me wrong.
60 His name is Licio, born in Mantua.

Baptista. You're welcome, sir, and he for your good sake.
But for my daughter Katharine, this I know,
She is not for your turn, the more my grief.
Petruchio. I see you do not mean to part with her,
Or else you like not of my company.
Baptista. Mistake me not, I speak but as I find.
Whence are you, sir? what may I call your name?
Petruchio. Petruchio is my name, Antonio's son,
A man well known throughout all Italy.
Baptista. I know him well: you are welcome for his sake. 70
Gremio. Saving your tale, Petruchio, I pray,
Let us, that are poor petitioners, speak too!
Backare! you are marvellous forward.
Petruchio. O, pardon me, Signior Gremio, I would fain be doing.
Gremio. I doubt it not, sir; but you will curse your wooing.
[*to Baptista*] Neighbour, this is a gift very grateful, I am sure of it. To express the like kindness, myself, that have been more kindly beholding to you than any, freely give unto you this young scholar, [*presenting Lucentio*] that hath been long studying at Rheims, as cunning in 80 Greek, Latin, and other languages, as the other in music and mathematics. His name is Cambio; pray accept his service.
Baptista. A thousand thanks, Signior Gremio: welcome, good Cambio. [*he turns to Tranio*] But, gentle sir, methinks you walk like a stranger. May I be so bold to know the cause of your coming?
Tranio. Pardon me, sir, the boldness is mine own,
That, being a stranger in this city here,
Do make myself a suitor to your daughter, 90

Unto Bianca, fair, and virtuous:
Nor is your firm resolve unknown to me,
In the preferment of the eldest sister.
This liberty is all that I request,
That, upon knowledge of my parentage,
I may have welcome 'mongst the rest that woo,
And free access and favour as the rest.
And toward the education of your daughters
I here bestow a simple instrument,
100 And this small packet of Greek and Latin books.
[*Biondello comes forward with lute and books*
If you accept them, then their worth is great.
Baptista. Lucentio is your name—of whence, I pray?
Tranio. Of Pisa, sir, son to Vincentio.
Baptista. A mighty man of Pisa—by report
I know him well: you are very welcome, sir.
Take you the lute, and you the set of books,
[*to Hortensio and Lucentio*
You shall go see your pupils presently.
Holla, within!
A servant enters
Sirrah, lead these gentlemen
To my daughters, and tell them both,
110 These are their tutors, bid them use them well.
[*Hortensio and Lucentio depart*
We will go walk a little in the orchard,
And then to dinner. You are passing welcome,
And so I pray you all to think yourselves.
Petruchio. Signior Baptista, my business asketh haste,
And every day I cannot come to woo.
You knew my father well, and in him me,
Left solely heir to all his lands and goods,

Which I have bettered rather than decreased,
Then tell me—if I get your daughter's love,
What dowry shall I have with her to wife? 120
Baptista. After my death, the one half of my lands,
And in possession twenty thousand crowns.
Petruchio. And, for that dowry, I'll assure her of
Her widowhood—be it that she survive me—
In all my lands and leases whatsoever.
Let specialties be therefore drawn between us,
That covenants may be kept on either hand.
Baptista. Ay, when the special thing is well obtained,
This is, her love; for that is all in all.
Petruchio. Why, that is nothing; for I tell you, father, 130
I am as peremptory as she proud-minded;
And where two raging fires meet together,
They do consume the thing that feeds their fury.
Though little fire grows great with little wind,
Yet extreme gusts will blow out fire and all:
So I to her, and so she yields to me.
For I am rough and woo not like a babe.
Baptista. Well mayst thou woo, and happy be
thy speed!
But be thou armed for some unhappy words.
Petruchio. Ay, to the proof—as mountains are for winds, 140
That shake not, though they blow perpetually.

'*Enters* HORTENSIO *with his head broke*'

Baptista. How now, my friend! why dost thou look
so pale?
Hortensio. For fear, I promise you, if I look pale.
Baptista. What, will my daughter prove a
good musician?
Hortensio. I think she'll sooner prove a soldier—
Iron may hold with her, but never lutes.

Baptista. Why, then thou canst not break her to the lute?

Hortensio. Why no, for she hath broke the lute to me.
I did but tell her she mistook her frets,
150 And bowed her hand to teach her fingering,
When, with a most impatient devilish spirit,
'Frets, call you these?' quoth she, 'I'll fume with them':
And, with that word, she struck me on the head,
And through the instrument my pate made way,
And there I stood amazéd for a while,
As on a pillory, looking through the lute.
While she did call me rascal fiddler,
And twangling Jack, with twenty such vile terms,
As had she studied to misuse me so.

160 *Petruchio.* Now, by the world, it is a lusty wench.
I love her ten times more than e'er I did,
O, how I long to have some chat with her!

Baptista. Well, go with me, and be not so discomfited
Proceed in practice with my younger daughter,
She's apt to learn and thankful for good turns.
Signior Petruchio, will you go with us,
Or shall I send my daughter Kate to you?

Petruchio. I pray you do. I will attend her here,
[*all depart save Petruchio*
And woo her with some spirit when she comes.
170 Say that she rail, why then I'll tell her plain
She sings as sweetly as a nightingale:
Say that she frown, I'll say she looks as clear
As morning roses newly washed with dew:
Say she be mute and will not speak a word,
Then I'll commend her volubility,
And say she uttereth piercing eloquence:
If she do bid me pack, I'll give her thanks,
As though she bid me stay by her a week:

If she deny to wed, I'll crave the day
When I shall ask the banns, and when be married. 180
But here she comes, and now, Petruchio, speak.

KATHARINA enters

Good morrow, Kate—for that's your name, I hear.
Katharina. Well have you heard, but something hard of hearing;
They call me Katharine that do talk of me.
Petruchio. You lie, in faith, for you are called plain Kate,
And bonny Kate, and sometimes Kate the curst:
But Kate, the prettiest Kate in Christendom,
Kate of Kate Hall, my super-dainty Kate,
For dainties are all cates, and therefore, Kate,
Take this of me, Kate of my consolation— 190
Hearing thy mildness praised in every town,
Thy virtues spoke of, and thy beauty sounded,
Yet not so deeply as to thee belongs,
Myself am moved to woo thee for my wife.
Katharina. Moved! in good time! let him that moved you hither,
Remove you hence: I knew you at the first
You were a moveable.
Petruchio. Why, what's a moveable?
Katharina. A joint-stool.
Petruchio. Thou hast hit it: come, sit on me.
Katharina. Asses are made to bear, and so are you.
Petruchio. Women are made to bear, and so are you. 200
Katharina. No such a jade as you, if me you mean.
Petruchio. Alas, good Kate! I will not burden thee,
For knowing thee to be but young and light,—
Katharina. Too light for such a swain as you to catch,
And yet as heavy as my weight should be.

Petruchio. Should be! should—buzz!
Katharina. Well ta'en, and like a buzzard.
Petruchio. O, slow-winged turtle! shall a buzzard take thee?
Katharina. Ay, for a turtle, as he takes a buzzard.
Petruchio. Come, come, you wasp, i'faith, you are too angry.
210 *Katharina.* If I be waspish, best beware my sting.
Petruchio. My remedy is then, to pluck it out.
Katharina. Ay, if the fool could find it where it lies.
Petruchio. Who knows not where a wasp doth wear his sting?
In his tail.
Katharina. In his tongue.
Petruchio. Whose tongue?
Katharina. Yours, if you talk of tales, and so farewell.
[*she turns to go*
Petruchio. What, with my tongue in your tail? nay, come again. [*he seizes her in his arms*
Good Kate, I am a gentleman—
Katharina. That I'll try.
['*she strikes him*'
Petruchio. I swear I'll cuff you, if you strike again.
Katharina. So may you loose your arms!
220 If you strike me, you are no gentleman,
And if no gentleman, why then no arms.
Petruchio. A herald, Kate? O, put me in thy books!
Katharina. What is your crest? a coxcomb?
Petruchio. A combless cock, so Kate will be my hen.
Katharina. No cock of mine, you crow too like a craven.
Petruchio. Nay, come, Kate, come; you must not look so sour.
Katharina. It is my fashion, when I see a crab.

Petruchio. Why, here's no crab, and therefore look not sour.

Katharina. There is, there is.

Petruchio. Then show it me.

Katharina. Had I a glass, I would. 230

Petruchio. What, you mean my face?

Katharina. Well aimed of such a young one.
[*she struggles*

Petruchio. Now, by S. George, I am too young for you.

Katharina. Yet you are withered.
[*touches his forehead*

Petruchio [*kisses her hand*]. 'Tis with cares.

Katharina [*she slips from him*]. I care not!

Petruchio. Nay, hear you, Kate. In sooth, you scape not so. [*he catches her once more*

Katharina. I chafe you, if I tarry. Let me go!
[*she struggles again, biting and scratching as he speaks*

Petruchio. No, not a whit—I find you passing gentle:
'Twas told me you were rough and coy and sullen,
And now I find report a very liar;
For thou art pleasant, gamesome, passing courteous,
But slow in speech; yet sweet as spring-time flowers. 240
Thou canst not frown, thou canst not look askance,
Nor bite the lip, as angry wenches will,
Nor hast thou pleasure to be cross in talk;
But thou with mildness entertain'st thy wooers,
With gentle conference, soft and affable....
[*he releases her*
Why does the world report that Kate doth limp?
O sland'rous world! Kate like the hazel-twig
Is straight and slender, and as brown in hue
As hazel-nuts and sweeter than the kernels...

250 O, let me see thee walk: thou dost not halt.
Katharina. Go, fool, and whom thou keep'st command.
Petruchio. Did ever Dian so become a grove
As Kate this chamber with her princely gait?
O, be thou Dian and let her be Kate,
And then let Kate be chaste and Dian sportful!
Katharina. Where did you study all this goodly speech?
Petruchio. It is extempore, from my mother-wit.
Katharina. A witty mother! witless else her son.
Petruchio. Am I not wise?
Katharina. Yes, keep you warm.
260 *Petruchio.* Marry, so I mean, sweet Katharine, in thy bed:
And therefore, setting all this chat aside,
Thus in plain terms: your father hath consented
That you shall be my wife; your dowry 'greed on;
And, will you, nill you, I will marry you.
Now, Kate, I am a husband for your turn,
For by this light whereby I see thy beauty,
Thy beauty that doth make me like thee well,
Thou must be married to no man but me.
For I am he am born to tame you, Kate,
270 And bring you from a wild Kate to a Kate
Conformable as other household Kates.

BAPTISTA, GREMIO, and TRANIO re-enter the room

Here comes your father—never make denial—
I must and will have Katharine to my wife.
Baptista. Now, Signior Petruchio, how speed you with my daughter?
Petruchio. How but well, sir? how but well?
It were impossible I should speed amiss.
Baptista. Why, how now, daughter Katharine! in your dumps?

Katharina. Call you me daughter? now, I promise you
You have showed a tender fatherly regard,
To wish me wed to one half lunatic, 280
A mad-cap ruffian and a swearing Jack,
That thinks with oaths to face the matter out.

Petruchio. Father, 'tis thus—yourself and all the world,
That talked of her, have talked amiss of her:
If she be curst, it is for policy:
For she's not froward, but modest as the dove;
She is not hot, but temperate as the morn;
For patience she will prove a second Grissel,
A Roman Lucrece for her chastity.
And to conclude, we have 'greed so well together, 290
That upon Sunday is the wedding-day.

Katharina. I'll see thee hanged on Sunday first.

Gremio. Hark, Petruchio, she says she'll see thee hanged first.

Tranio. Is this your speeding? nay, then, good night our part!

Petruchio. Be patient, gentlemen, I choose her for myself—
If she and I be pleased, what's that to you?
'Tis bargained 'twixt us twain, being alone,
That she shall still be curst in company.
I tell you, 'tis incredible to believe
How much she loves me: O, the kindest Kate! 300
She hung about my neck, and kiss on kiss
She vied so fast, protesting oath on oath,
That in a twink she won me to her love.
O, you are novices! 'tis a world to see,
How tame, when men and women are alone,
A meacock wretch can make the curstest shrew.
[*he snatches her hand*
Give me thy hand, Kate, I will unto Venice,

To buy apparel 'gainst the wedding-day...
Provide the feast, father, and bid the guests,
310 I will be sure my Katharine shall be fine.

Baptista. I know not what to say—but give me your hands.
God send you joy, Petruchio! 'tis a match.

Gremio, Tranio. Amen, say we. We will be witnesses.

Petruchio. Father, and wife, and gentlemen, adieu,
I will to Venice—Sunday comes apace—
We will have rings, and things, and fine array,
And kiss me, Kate, we will be married o' Sunday.

[*he seizes her in his arms and kisses her; she breaks from him and flies the room; he departs by another door*

Gremio. Was ever match clapped up so suddenly?

Baptista. Faith, gentlemen, now I play a merchant's part,
320 And venture madly on a desperate mart.

Tranio. 'Twas a commodity lay fretting by you,
'Twill bring you gain, or perish on the seas.

Baptista. The gain I seek is quiet in the match.

Gremio. No doubt but he hath got a quiet catch.
But now, Baptista, to your younger daughter—
Now is the day we long have lookéd for.
I am your neighbour, and was suitor first.

Tranio. And I am one, that love Bianca more
Than words can witness, or your thoughts can guess.

330 *Gremio.* Youngling! thou canst not love so dear as I.

Tranio. Greybeard! thy love doth freeze.

Gremio. But thine doth fry.
Skipper, stand back—'tis age that nourisheth.

Tranio. But youth in ladies' eyes that flourisheth.

Baptista. Content you, gentlemen, I will compound this strife.
'Tis deeds must win the prize, and he, of both,

That can assure my daughter greatest dower,
Shall have Bianca's love.
Say, Signior Gremio, what can you assure her?
Gremio. First, as you know, my house within the city
Is richly furnishéd with plate and gold, 340
Basins and ewers to lave her dainty hands;
My hangings all of Tyrian tapestry;
In ivory coffers I have stuffed my crowns;
In cypress chests my arras counterpoints,
Costly apparel, tents, and canopies,
Fine linen, Turkey cushions bossed with pearl,
Valance of Venice gold in needlework,
Pewter and brass, and all things that belong
To house or housekeeping. Then, at my farm
I have a hundred milch-kine to the pail, 350
Sixscore fat oxen standing in my stalls,
And all things answerable to this portion.
Myself am struck in years, I must confess,
And if I die to-morrow this is hers,
If whilst I live she will be only mine.
Tranio. That 'only' came well in. Sir, list to me,
I am my father's heir and only son.
If I may have your daughter to my wife,
I'll leave her houses three or four as good,
Within rich Pisa walls, as any one 360
Old Signior Gremio has in Padua,
Besides two thousand ducats by the year
Of fruitful land, all which shall be her jointure.
What, have I pinched you, Signior Gremio?
Gremio. Two thousand ducats by the year, of land!
[*aside*] My land amounts not to so much in all.
That she shall have—besides an argosy
That now is lying in Marseilles' road.
What, have I choked you with an argosy?

370 *Tranio.* Gremio, 'tis known my father hath no less
Than three great argosies, besides two galliasses,
And twelve tight galleys. These I will assure her,
And twice as much, whate'er thou offer'st next.
Gremio. Nay, I have offered all, I have no more,
And she can have no more than all I have.
If you like me, she shall have me and mine.
Tranio. Why, then the maid is mine from all the world,
By your firm promise—Gremio is out-vied.
Baptista. I must confess your offer is the best,
380 And, let your father make her the assurance,
She is your own—else, you must pardon me,
If you should die before him, where's her dower?
Tranio. That's but a cavil; he is old, I young.
Gremio. And may not young men die, as well as old?
Baptista. Well, gentlemen,
I am thus resolved—On Sunday next you know
My daughter Katharine is to be married:
Now, on the Sunday following, shall Bianca
Be bride to you, if you make this assurance;
390 If not, to Signior Gremio:
And so I take my leave, and thank you both.
[*he bows and departs*
Gremio. Adieu, good neighbour. Now I fear thee not;
Sirrah, young gamester, your father were a fool
To give thee all, and in his waning age
Set foot under thy table: tut, a toy!
An old Italian fox is not so kind, my boy. [*he goes*
Tranio. A vengeance on your crafty withered hide!
Yet I have faced it with a card of ten.
'Tis in my head to do my master good:
400 I see no reason but supposed Lucentio
Must get a father, called—supposed Vincentio.

And that's a wonder: fathers commonly
Do get their children; but, in this case of wooing,
A child shall get a sire, if I fail not of my cunning.
[*he goes*

[3. 1.] *Bianca's room in the house of Baptista*

BIANCA and HORTENSIO, disguised as Licio, are seated with a lute; LUCENTIO, disguised as Cambio, standing a little apart, waiting his turn. HORTENSIO takes BIANCA's hand in his to teach her fingering

Lucentio [*interrupts*]. Fiddler, forbear, you grow too forward, sir!
Have you so soon forgot the entertainment
Her sister Katharine welcomed you withal?
Hortensio. But, wrangling pedant, this is
The patroness of heavenly harmony:
Then give me leave to have prerogative,
And when in music we have spent an hour,
Your lecture shall have leisure for as much.
Lucentio. Preposterous ass, that never read so far
To know the cause why music was ordained! 10
Was it not to refresh the mind of man
After his studies or his usual pain?
Then give me leave to read philosophy,
And while I pause, serve in your harmony.
Hortensio [*rises*]. Sirrah, I will not bear these braves of thine.
Bianca [*comes between them*]. Why, gentlemen, you do me double wrong,
To strive for that which resteth in my choice:
I am no breeching scholar in the schools,
I'll not be tied to hours nor 'pointed times,
But learn my lessons as I please myself. 20

And, to cut off all strife, here sit we down:
Take you your instrument, play you the whiles—
His lecture will be done ere you have tuned.

Hortensio. You'll leave his lecture when I am in tune?

Lucentio. That will be never! [*Hortensio threatens*] Tune your instrument.

[*Hortensio angrily withdraws; Bianca and Lucentio sit*

Bianca. Where left we last?

Lucentio. Here, madam:
'Hic ibat Simois, hic est Sigeia tellus,
Hic steterat Priami regia celsa senis.'

30 *Bianca.* Construe them.

Lucentio. 'Hic ibat,' as I told you before—'Simois,' I am Lucentio—'hic est,' son unto Vincentio of Pisa—'Sigeia tellus,' disguised thus to get your love—'Hic steterat,' and that Lucentio that comes a-wooing—'Priami,' is my man Tranio—'regia,' bearing my port—'celsa senis,' that we might beguile the old pantaloon.

Hortensio [*returns*]. Madam, my instrument's in tune.

Bianca. Let's hear—[*he plays*] O fie! the treble jars.

40 *Lucentio.* Spit in the hole, man, and tune again.

[*Hortensio once more withdraws*

Bianca. Now let me see if I can construe it. 'Hic ibat Simois,' I know you not—'hic est Sigeia tellus,' I trust you not—'Hic steterat Priami,' take heed he hear us not—'regia,' presume not—'celsa senis,' despair not.

Hortensio [*returns again*]. Madam, 'tis now in tune.

Lucentio. All but the base.

Hortensio. The base is right, 'tis the base knave, that jars.

[*aside*] How fiery and forward our pedant is!
Now, for my life, the knave doth court my love.
Pedascule, I'll watch you better yet. 50
[*he steals behind them*

Bianca. In time I may believe, yet I mistrust.

Lucentio. Mistrust it not—[*perceives Hortensio*] for, sure, Æacides
Was Ajax, called so from his grandfather.

Bianca [*rises*]. I must believe my master, else, I promise you,
I should be arguing still upon that doubt—
But let it rest. Now, Licio, to you.
[*she leads him aside*
Good master, take it not unkindly, pray,
That I have been thus pleasant with you both.

Hortensio [*over his shoulder*]. You may go walk, and give me leave awhile—
My lessons make no music in three parts. 60

Lucentio. Are you so formal, sir? well, I must wait—
[*aside*] And watch withal, for, but I be deceived,
Our fine musician groweth amorous.
[*he withdraws a little; Hortensio and Bianca sit*

Hortensio. Madam, before you touch the instrument,
To learn the order of my fingering,
I must begin with rudiments of art,
To teach you gamut in a briefer sort,
More pleasant, pithy, and effectual,
Than hath been taught by any of my trade:
And there it is in writing, fairly drawn. 70

Bianca. Why, I am past my gamut long ago.

Hortensio. Yet read the gamut of Hortensio.

Bianca [*reads*]. ''Gamut' I am, the ground of all accord;

'A re,' to plead Hortensio's passion;
'B mi,' Bianca, take him for thy lord,
'C fa ut,' that loves with all affection:
'D sol re,' one clef, two notes have I,
'E la mi,' show pity, or I die.'
Call you this gamut? tut! I like it not.
80 Old fashions please me best—I am not so nice
To change true rules for odd inventions.

A servant enters

Servant. Mistress, your father prays you leave your books,
And help to dress your sister's chamber up.
You know to-morrow is the wedding-day.

Bianca. Farewell sweet masters both, I must be gone. [*she departs*

Lucentio. Faith, mistress, then I have no cause to stay. [*he goes*

Hortensio. But I have cause to pry into this pedant,
Methinks he looks as though he were in love:
Yet if thy thoughts, Bianca, be so humble,
90 To cast thy wandring eyes on every stale,
Seize thee that list—if once I find thee ranging,
Hortensio will be quit with thee by changing. [*he goes*

[3. 2.] *The public square*

BAPTISTA, GREMIO, TRANIO (*as Lucentio*), LUCENTIO (*as Cambio*), KATHARINA (*in bridal array*), BIANCA, *attendants and a concourse of people*

Baptista [*to Tranio*]. Signior Lucentio, this is the 'pointed day,
That Katharine and Petruchio should be married,
And yet we hear not of our son-in-law:

What will be said? what mockery will it be,
To want the bridegroom when the priest attends
To speak the ceremonial rites of marriage?
What says Lucentio to this shame of ours?

Katharina. No shame but mine. I must forsooth be forced
To give my hand opposed against my heart
Unto a mad-brain rudesby, full of spleen, 10
Who wooed in haste, and means to wed at leisure...
I told you, I, he was a frantic fool,
Hiding his bitter jests in blunt behaviour:
And to be noted for a merry man,
He'll woo a thousand, 'point the day of marriage,
†Make feasts, invite friends, and proclaim the banns,
Yet never means to wed where he hath wooed.
Now must the world point at poor Katharine,
And say, 'Lo, there is mad Petruchio's wife,
If it would please him come and marry her.' 20

Tranio. Patience, good Katharine, and Baptista too.
Upon my life, Petruchio means but well,
Whatever fortune stays him from his word.
Though he be blunt, I know him passing wise,
Though he be merry, yet withal he's honest.

Katharina. Would Katharine had never seen him though!

[*she turns homeward 'weeping,' followed by Bianca and the rest of the bridal train*

Baptista. Go, girl, I cannot blame thee now to weep,
For such an injury would vex a saint,
Much more a shrew of thy impatient humour.

BIONDELLO comes running up

Biondello. Master, master! news, and such old news 30
as you never heard of!

Baptista. Is it new and old too? how may that be?

Biondello. Why, is it not news, to hear of Petruchio's coming?

Baptista. Is he come?

Biondello. Why, no, sir.

Baptista. What then?

Biondello. He is coming.

Baptista. When will he be here?

40 *Biondello.* When he stands where I am and sees you there.

Tranio. But say, what to thine old news?

Biondello. Why, Petruchio is coming, in a new hat and an old jerkin; a pair of old breeches thrice turned; a pair of boots that have been candle-cases, one buckled, another laced; an old rusty sword ta'en out of the town-armoury, with a broken hilt, and chapeless; with two broken points: †with an old mothy saddle and stirrups of no kindred: his horse hipped besides, possessed with 50 the glanders and like to mose in the chine, troubled with the lampass, infected with the fashions, full of windgalls, sped with spavins, rayed with the yellows, past cure of the fives, stark spoiled with the staggers, begnawn with the bots, swayed in the back, and shoulder-shotten, near-legged before, and with a half-checked bit, and a head-stall of sheep's leather, which, being restrained to keep him from stumbling, hath been often burst and new-repaired with knots: one girth six times pieced, and a woman's crupper of velure, which 60 hath two letters for her name, fairly set down in studs, and here and there pieced with pack-thread.

Baptista. Who comes with him?

Biondello. O, sir, his lackey, for all the world caparisoned like the horse: with a linen stock on one leg, and a kersey boot-hose on the other, gartered with a red and blue list; an old hat, and the humour of forty fancies pricked in't for a feather; a monster, a very monster in apparel, and not like a Christian footboy or a gentleman's lackey.

Tranio. 'Tis some odd humour pricks him to this fashion. 70
Yet oftentimes he goes but mean-apparelled.

Baptista. I am glad he's come, howsoe'er he comes.

Biondello. Why, sir, he comes not.

Baptista. Didst thou not say he comes?

Biondello. Who? that Petruchio came?

Baptista. Ay, that Petruchio came.

Biondello. No, sir, I say his horse comes, with him on his back.

Baptista. Why, that's all one.

Biondello. Nay, by S. Jamy, 80
I hold you a penny,
A horse and a man
Is more than one,
And yet not many.

PETRUCHIO and GRUMIO, basely attired, enter the square in boisterous fashion

Petruchio. Come, where be these gallants? who's at home?

Baptista [*coldly*]. You are welcome, sir.

Petruchio. And yet I come not well?

Baptista. And yet you halt not.

Tranio. Not so well apparelled
As I wish you were.

Petruchio. Were it not better I should rush in thus?
But where is Kate? where is my lovely bride? 90
How does my father? Gentles, methinks you frown
And wherefore gaze this goodly company,

As if they saw some wondrous monument,
Some comet, or unusual prodigy?

Baptista. Why, sir, you know, this is your wedding-day:
First were we sad, fearing you would not come,
Now sadder, that you come so unprovided.
Fie! doff this habit, shame to your estate,
An eyesore to our solemn festival.

100 *Tranio.* And tell us what occasion of import
Hath all so long detained you from your wife,
And sent you hither so unlike yourself?

Petruchio. Tedious it were to tell, and harsh to hear—
Sufficeth I am come to keep my word,
Though in some part enforcéd to digress,
Which at more leisure I will so excuse
As you shall well be satisfied withal.
But where is Kate? I stay too long from her,
The morning wears, 'tis time we were at church.

110 *Tranio.* See not your bride in these unreverent robes,
Go to my chamber, put on clothes of mine.

Petruchio. Not I, believe me—thus I'll visit her.

Baptista. But thus, I trust, you will not marry her.

Petruchio. Good sooth, even thus: therefore ha' done with words,
To me she's married, not unto my clothes:
Could I repair what she will wear in me,
As I can change these poor accoutrements,
'Twere well for Kate, and better for myself.
But what a fool am I to chat with you,
120 When I should bid good morrow to my bride,
And seal the title with a lovely kiss.

[*he hastens off with Grumio behind him*

Tranio. He hath some meaning in his mad attire.
We will persuade him, be it possible,

To put on better ere he go to church.
Baptista. I'll after him, and see the event of this.
[*he follows Petruchio; Gremio and others also depart*
Tranio. But to her love concerneth us to add
Her father's liking, which to bring to pass,
As I before imparted to your worship,
I am to get a man—whate'er he be,
It skills not much, we'll fit him to our turn— 130
And he shall be Vincentio of Pisa,
And make assurance here in Padua
Of greater sums than I have promiséd.
So shall you quietly enjoy your hope,
And marry sweet Bianca with consent.
Lucentio. Were it not that my fellow-schoolmaster
Doth watch Bianca's steps so narrowly,
'Twere good methinks to steal our marriage,
Which once performed, let all the world say no,
I'll keep mine own despite of all the world. 140
Tranio. That by degrees we mean to look into,
And watch our vantage in this business.
We'll over-reach the greybeard, Gremio,
The narrow-prying father, Minola,
The quaint musician, amorous Licio—
All for my master's sake, Lucentio.

GREMIO returns

Signior Gremio, came you from the church?
Gremio. As willingly as e'er I came from school.
Tranio. And is the bride and bridegroom coming home?
Gremio. A bridegroom, say you? 'tis a groom, indeed, 150
A grumbling groom, and that the girl shall find.
Tranio. Curster than she? why, 'tis impossible.

Gremio. Why, he's a devil, a devil, a very fiend.
Tranio. Why, she's a devil, a devil, the devil's dam.
Gremio. Tut! she's a lamb, a dove, a fool to him...
I'll tell you, Sir Lucentio: when the priest
Should ask if Katharine should be his wife,
'Ay, by gogs-wouns,' quoth he, and swore so loud,
That all-amazed the priest let fall the book,
160 And as he stooped again to take it up,
This mad-brained bridegroom took him such a cuff,
That down fell priest and book, and book and priest.
'Now take them up,' quoth he, 'if any list.'
Tranio. What said the wench, when he arose again?
Gremio. Trembled and shook; for why, he stamped and swore,
As if the vicar meant to cozen him.
But after many ceremonies done,
He calls for wine—'A health,' quoth he, as if
He had been aboard, carousing to his mates
170 After a storm—quaffed off the muscadel,
And threw the sops all in the sexton's face;
Having no other reason
But that his beard grew thin and hungerly,
And seemed to ask him sops as he was drinking.
This done, he took the bride about the neck,
And kissed her lips with such a clamorous smack,
That at the parting all the church did echo:
And I seeing this came thence for very shame,
And after me, I know, the rout is coming.
180 Such a mad marriage never was before:
Hark, hark! I hear the minstrels play.

The minstrels with the marriage procession enter the square, PETRUCHIO *and* KATHARINA *leading, followed by* BIANCA, BAPTISTA, HORTENSIO, GRUMIO, *and the rest of their train*

Petruchio. Gentlemen and friends, I thank you for your pains,
I know you think to dine with me to-day,
And have prepared great store of wedding cheer,
But so it is, my haste doth call me hence,
And therefore here I mean to take my leave.
Baptista. Is't possible you will away to-night?
Petruchio. I must away to-day before night come.
Make it no wonder; if you knew my business,
You would entreat me rather go than stay. 190
And, honest company, I thank you all,
That have beheld me give away myself
To this most patient, sweet, and virtuous wife.
Dine with my father, drink a health to me,
For I must hence, and farewell to you all.
Tranio. Let us entreat you stay till after dinner.
Petruchio. It may not be.
Gremio. Let me entreat you.
Petruchio. It cannot be.
Katharina. Let me entreat you.
Petruchio. I am content.
Katharina. Are you content to stay?
Petruchio. I am content you shall entreat me stay— 200
But yet not stay, entreat me how you can.
Katharina. Now, if you love me, stay.
Petruchio. Grumio, my horse.
Grumio. Ay, sir, they be ready—the oats have eaten the horses.
Katharina. Nay, then,
Do what thou canst, I will not go to-day,
No, nor to-morrow, till I please myself.
The door is open, sir, there lies your way,
You may be jogging whiles your boots are green;
For me, I'll not be gone, till I please myself. 210

'Tis like you'll prove a jolly, surly groom,
That take it on you at the first so roundly.
Petruchio. O, Kate, content thee, prithee, be not angry.
Katharina. I will be angry—what hast thou to do?
Father, be quiet—he shall stay my leisure.
Gremio. Ay, marry, sir, now it begins to work.
Katharina. Gentlemen, forward to the bridal dinner.
I see a woman may be made a fool,
If she had not a spirit to resist.
220 *Petruchio* [*fiercely*]. They shall go forward, Kate, at thy command.
Obey the bride, you that attend on her!
Go to the feast, revel and domineer,
Carouse full measure to her maidenhead,
Be mad and merry, or go hang yourselves;
But for my bonny Kate, she must with me.
[*he takes her about the waist, as in defiance of the company*
Nay, look not big, nor stamp, nor stare, nor fret,
I will be master of what is mine own.
She is my goods, my chattels; she is my house,
My household stuff, my field, my barn,
230 My horse, my ox, my ass, my any thing—
And here she stands, touch her whoever dare!
I'll bring mine action on the proudest he
That stops my way in Padua. Grumio,
Draw forth thy weapon, we are beset with thieves,
Rescue thy mistress, if thou be a man.
Fear not, sweet wench, they shall not touch thee, Kate!
I'll buckler thee against a million.
[*he carries her from the square, Grumio making pretence to cover his retreat*
Baptista. Nay, let them go, a couple of quiet ones.
Gremio. Went they not quickly, I should die with laughing.

Tranio. Of all mad matches never was the like! 240

Lucentio. Mistress, what's your opinion of your sister?

Bianca. That, being mad herself, she's madly mated.

Gremio. I warrant him, Petruchio is Kated.

Baptista. Neighbours and friends, though bride and bridegroom wants
For to supply the places at the table,
You know, there wants no junkets at the feast.
Lucentio, you shall supply the bridegroom's place,
And let Bianca take her sister's room.

Tranio. Shall sweet Bianca practise how to bride it?
[*he takes her hand*

Baptista. She shall, Lucentio. Come, gentlemen, 250
let's go. [*they go in*

[4. 1.] *The hall of Petruchio's house in the country; stairs leading to a gallery; a large open hearth; a table, benches, and stools; three doors, one opening on to the porch without*

GRUMIO *enters the house, his shoulders covered with snow, his legs with mud*

Grumio [*throws himself upon a bench*]. Fie, fie, on all tired jades, on all mad masters, and all foul ways! Was ever man so beaten? was ever man so rayed? was ever man so weary? I am sent before to make a fire, and they are coming after to warm them. Now, were not I a little pot, and soon hot, my very lips might freeze to my teeth, my tongue to the roof of my mouth, my heart in my belly, ere I should come by a fire to thaw me. But I, with blowing the fire, shall warm myself; for, considering the weather, a taller man than I will take cold. 10
Holla, ho! Curtis!

CURTIS enters

Curtis. Who is that calls so coldly?

Grumio. A piece of ice: if thou doubt it, thou mayst slide from my shoulder to my heel with no greater a run but my head and my neck. A fire, good Curtis.

Curtis. Is my master and his wife coming, Grumio?

Grumio. O, ay, Curtis, ay—and therefore fire, fire; cast on no water.

Curtis. Is she so hot a shrew as she's reported?

20 *Grumio.* She was, good Curtis, before this frost: but thou know'st winter tames man, woman, and beast; for it hath tamed my old master, and my new mistress, and myself, fellow Curtis.

Curtis. Away, you three-inch fool! I am no beast.

Grumio. Am I but three inches? why, thy horn is a foot, and so long am I at the least. But wilt thou make a fire, or shall I complain on thee to our mistress, whose hand (she being now at hand) thou shalt soon feel, to thy cold comfort, for being slow in thy hot office?

30 *Curtis* [*sets about kindling a fire on the hearth*]. I prithee, good Grumio, tell me, how goes the world?

Grumio. A cold world, Curtis, in every office but thine—and therefore fire. Do thy duty, and have thy duty, for my master and mistress are almost frozen to death.

Curtis [*rises from the hearth*]. There's fire ready, and therefore, good Grumio, the news?

Grumio. Why, 'Jack boy! ho boy!' and as much news as thou wilt.

40 *Curtis.* Come, you are so full of cony-catching.

Grumio [*warms his hands*]. Why therefore fire, for I have caught extreme cold. Where's the cook? is supper ready, the house trimmed, rushes strewed, cobwebs swept, the serving-men in their new fustian, their white stockings, and every officer his wedding-garment on? Be the jacks fair within, the jills fair without, the carpets laid, and every thing in order?

Curtis. All ready: and therefore, I pray thee, news.

Grumio. First, know, my horse is tired, my master and mistress fallen out— 50

Curtis. How?

Grumio. Out of their saddles into the dirt, and thereby hangs a tale.

Curtis. Let's ha't, good Grumio.

Grumio. Lend thine ear.

Curtis. Here.

Grumio. There. [*he strikes him*

Curtis. This is to feel a tale, not to hear a tale.

Grumio. And therefore 'tis called, a sensible tale: and this cuff was but to knock at your ear and beseech 60 listening: now I begin—Imprimis, we came down a foul hill, my master riding behind my mistress—

Curtis. Both of one horse?

Grumio. What's that to thee?

Curtis. Why, a horse.

Grumio. Tell thou the tale: but hadst thou not crossed me, thou shouldst have heard how her horse fell, and she under her horse; thou shouldst have heard in how miry a place, how she was bemoiled, how he left her with the horse upon her, how he beat me because her 70 horse stumbled, how she waded through the dirt to pluck him off me; how he swore, how she prayed that never prayed before; how I cried, how the horses ran away, how her bridle was burst; how I lost my crupper —with many things of worthy memory, which now shall die in oblivion, and thou return unexperienced to thy grave.

Curtis. By this reck'ning he is more shrew than she.

Grumio. Ay, and that thou and the proudest of you all
80 shall find when he comes home. But what talk I of this? Call forth Nathaniel, Joseph, Nicholas, Philip, Walter Sugarsop, and the rest; let their heads be sleekly combed, their blue coats brushed, and their garters of an indifferent knit; let them curtsy with their left legs, and not presume to touch a hair of my master's horse-tail, till they kiss their hands. Are they all ready?

Curtis. They are.

Grumio. Call them forth.

Curtis [*calls*]. Do you hear, ho? you must meet my
90 master to countenance my mistress.

Grumio. Why, she hath a face of her own.

Curtis. Who knows not that?

Grumio. Thou, it seems, that calls for company to countenance her.

Curtis. I call them forth to credit her.

Grumio. Why, she comes to borrow nothing of them.

'*Enter four or five serving-men*'; *they crowd about Grumio*

Nathaniel. Welcome home, Grumio.

Philip. How now, Grumio!

Joseph. What, Grumio!

100 *Nicholas.* Fellow Grumio!

Nathaniel. How now, old lad?

Grumio. Welcome, you!—how now, you!—what, you!—fellow, you!—and thus much for greeting. Now, my spruce companions, is all ready, and all things neat?

Nathaniel. All things is ready. How near is our master?

Grumio. E'en at hand, alighted by this; and therefore be not——Cock's passion, silence! I hear my master.

The door is rudely flung open and PETRUCHIO *enters with* KATHARINA, *both stained with mire from head to foot; he strides into the midst of the room; she, well-nigh swooning but still untamed, stands leaning against the wall just within the door*

Petruchio. Where be these knaves? What, no man at the door,
To hold my stirrup, nor to take my horse! 110
Where is Nathaniel, Gregory, Philip?—
Servants [*running up*]. Here, here, sir—here, sir.
Petruchio. Here, sir! here, sir! here, sir! here, sir!—
You logger-headed and unpolished grooms!
What, no attendance? no regard? no duty?—
Where is the foolish knave I sent before?
Grumio. Here, sir, as foolish as I was before.
Petruchio. You peasant swain! you whoreson malt-horse drudge!
Did I not bid thee meet me in the park,
And bring along these rascal knaves with thee? 120
Grumio. Nathaniel's coat, sir, was not fully made,
And Gabriel's pumps were all unpinked i'th' heel;
There was no link to colour Peter's hat,
And Walter's dagger was not come from sheathing:
There were none fine but Adam, Rafe, and Gregory—
The rest were ragged, old, and beggarly.
Yet, as they are, here are they come to meet you.
Petruchio. Go, rascals, go, and fetch my supper in.
[*they hurry out*
[*he sings*] 'Where is the life that late I led'—
Where are those——[*perceiving Katharina still at the door*] Sit down, Kate, and welcome [*he brings her to the fire*]. Food, food, food, food! 130

'*Enter servants with supper*'

Why, when, I say? Nay, good sweet Kate, be merry.

[*he sits beside her*

Off with my boots, you rogues! you villains, when?

[*a servant kneels to take off his boots*

[*he sings*] 'It was the friar of orders grey,

As he forth walkéd on his way'—

Out, you rogue! you pluck my foot awry.

[*he strikes him*

Take that, and mend the plucking off the other.

[*the second boot is removed; he rises*

Be merry, Kate. Some water, here: what, ho!

['*Enter one with water*'; *Petruchio looks away*

140 Where's my spaniel Troilus? Sirrah, get you hence,

And bid my cousin Ferdinand come hither.

[*a servant goes out*

One, Kate, that you must kiss, and be acquainted with.

Where are my slippers? Shall I have some water?

[*the basin is a second time presented to him*

Come, Kate, and wash, and welcome heartily.

[*he stumbles against the servant and spills the water*

You whoreson villain! will you let it fall?

[*he strikes him*

Katharina. Patience, I pray you, 'twas a fault unwilling.

Petruchio. A whoreson, beetle-headed, flap-eared knave!

Come, Kate, sit down, I know you have a stomach.

[*she comes to the table*

Will you give thanks, sweet Kate, or else shall I?—

150 What's this? mutton?

1 Servant. Ay.

Petruchio. Who brought it?

Peter. I.

Petruchio. 'Tis burnt, and so is all the meat:

What dogs are these! Where is the rascal cook?
How durst you, villains, bring it from the dresser,
And serve it thus to me that love it not?
There, take it to you, trenchers, cups and all:
[he throws the meal at the servants' heads
You heedless joltheads, and unmannered slaves!
What, do you grumble? I'll be with you straight.
[he chases them all, save Curtis, from the room
Katharina. I pray you, husband, be not so disquiet,
The meat was well, if you were so contented.
Petruchio. I tell thee, Kate, 'twas burnt and dried away, 160
And I expressly am forbid to touch it:
For it engenders choler, planteth anger,
And better 'twere that both of us did fast—
Since, of ourselves, ourselves are choleric—
Than feed it with such over-roasted flesh.
Be patient, to-morrow't shall be mended,
And, for this night, we'll fast for company.
Come, I will bring thee to thy bridal chamber.
[they go upstairs, followed by Curtis; the servants return 'severally,' by stealth
Nathaniel. Peter, didst ever see the like?
Peter. He kills her in her own humour. 170

CURTIS comes down

Grumio. Where is he?
Curtis. In her chamber, making a sermon of continency to her,
And rails and swears and rates, that she, poor soul,
Knows not which way to stand, to look, to speak,
And sits as one new-risen from a dream.
Away, away! for he is coming hither.
[they fly from the room

PETRUCHIO appears in the gallery

Petruchio. Thus have I politicly begun my reign,
And 'tis my hope to end successfully:
180 My falcon now is sharp and passing empty,
And till she stoop, she must not be full-gorged,
For then she never looks upon her lure.
Another way I have to man my haggard,
To make her come and know her keeper's call:
That is, to watch her, as we watch these kites
That bate and beat and will not be obedient.
She eat no meat to-day, nor none shall eat;
Last night she slept not, nor to-night she shall not;
As with the meat, some undeservéd fault
190 I'll find about the making of the bed,
And here I'll fling the pillow, there the bolster,
This way the coverlet, another way the sheets:
Ay, and amid this hurly I intend
That all is done in reverend care of her.
And, in conclusion, she shall watch all night,
And, if she chance to nod, I'll rail and brawl,
And with the clamour keep her still awake.
This is a way to kill a wife with kindness;
And thus I'll curb her mad and headstrong humour.
200 He that knows better how to tame a shrew,
Now let him speak—'tis charity to show.
[*he returns to the bridal chamber*

[4. 2.] *The public square in Padua*

LUCENTIO (as Cambio) and BIANCA seated beneath the trees reading a book; TRANIO (as Lucentio) and HORTENSIO come from a house the other side of the square

Tranio. Is't possible, friend Licio, that Mistress Bianca
Doth fancy any other but Lucentio?
I tell you, sir, she bears me fair in hand.
Hortensio. Sir, to satisfy you in what I have said,
Stand by, and mark the manner of his teaching.
[*they stand behind a tree*
Lucentio. Now, mistress, profit you in what you read?
Bianca. What, master, read you? first resolve me that.
Lucentio. I read that I profess, the Art to Love.
Bianca. And may you prove, sir, master of your art!
Lucentio. While you, sweet dear, prove mistress of my heart. [*they kiss* 10
Hortensio. Quick proceeders, marry! Now, tell me, I pray,
You that durst swear that your mistress Bianca
Loved none in the world so well as Lucentio.
Tranio. O despiteful love! unconstant womankind!
I tell thee, Licio, this is wonderful.
Hortensio. Mistake no more, I am not Licio,
Nor a musician, as I seem to be,
But one that scorn to live in this disguise,
For such a one as leaves a gentleman,
And makes a god of such a cullion: 20
Know, sir, that I am called Hortensio.
Tranio. Signior Hortensio, I have often heard
Of your entire affection to Bianca,

And since mine eyes are witness of her lightness,
I will with you, if you be so contented,
Forswear Bianca and her love for ever.
Hortensio. See, how they kiss and court!
Signior Lucentio,
Here is my hand, and here I firmly vow
Never to woo her more, but do forswear her,
30 As one unworthy all the former favours
That I have fondly flattered her withal.
Tranio. And here I take the like unfeignéd oath,
Never to marry with her, though she would entreat.
Fie on her! see, how beastly she doth court him.
Hortensio. Would all the world but he had
quite forsworn!
For me, that I may surely keep mine oath,
I will be married to a wealthy widow,
Ere three days pass, which hath as long loved me
As I have loved this proud disdainful haggard.
40 And so farewell, Signior Lucentio.
Kindness in women, not their beauteous looks,
Shall win my love—and so I take my leave,
In resolution as I swore before.
[*he goes; Tranio joins the lovers*
Tranio. Mistress Bianca, bless you with such grace
As 'longeth to a lover's blesséd case!
Nay, I have ta'en you napping, gentle love,
And have forsworn you, with Hortensio.
Bianca. Tranio, you jest—but have you both
forsworn me?
Tranio. Mistress, we have.
Lucentio. Then we are rid of Licio.
50 *Tranio.* I'faith, he'll have a lusty widow now,
That shall be wooed and wedded in a day.
Bianca. God give him joy!

Tranio. Ay, and he'll tame her.
Bianca. He says so, Tranio.
Tranio. Faith, he is gone unto the taming-school.
Bianca. The taming-school! what, is there such a place?
Tranio. Ay, mistress, and Petruchio is the master,
That teacheth tricks eleven and twenty long,
To tame a shrew and charm her chattering tongue.

BIONDELLO runs up

Biondello. O master, master, I have watched so long
That I am dog-weary, but at last I spied 60
An ancient angel coming down the hill,
Will serve the turn.
Tranio. What is he, Biondello?
Biondello. Master, a mercatantè, or a pedant,
I know not what—but formal in apparel,
In gait and countenance surely like a father.
Lucentio. And what of him, Tranio?
Tranio. If he be credulous, and trust my tale,
I'll make him glad to seem Vincentio,
And give assurance to Baptista Minola,
As if he were the right Vincentio. 70
Take in your love, and then let me alone.
[*Lucentio and Bianca enter the house of Baptista*

The Pedant comes up

Pedant. God save you, sir!
Tranio. And you, sir! you are welcome.
Travel you far on, or are you at the farthest?
Pedant. Sir, at the farthest for a week or two,
But then up farther, and as far as Rome,
And so to Tripoli, if God lend me life.
Tranio. What countryman, I pray?
Pedant. Of Mantua.

Tranio. Of Mantua, sir? marry, God forbid!
And come to Padua, careless of your life?
80 *Pedant.* My life, sir! how, I pray? for that goes hard.
Tranio. 'Tis death for any one in Mantua
To come to Padua. Know you not the cause?
Your ships are stayed at Venice, and the duke—
For private quarrel 'twixt your duke and him—
Hath published and proclaimed it openly:
'Tis marvel, but that you are newly come,
You might have heard it else proclaimed about.
Pedant. Alas, sir, it is worse for me than so!
For I have bills for money by exchange
90 From Florence, and must here deliver them.
Tranio. Well, sir, to do you courtesy,
This will I do, and this I will advise you—
First, tell me, have you ever been at Pisa?
Pedant. Ay, sir, in Pisa have I often been,
Pisa renownéd for grave citizens.
Tranio. Among them know you one Vincentio?
Pedant. I know him not, but I have heard of him;
A merchant of incomparable wealth.
Tranio. He is my father, sir, and sooth to say,
100 In count'nance somewhat doth resemble you.
(*Biondello.* As much as an apple doth an oyster, and all one.
Tranio. To save your life in this extremity,
This favour will I do you for his sake—
And think it not the worst of all your fortunes
That you are like to Sir Vincentio—
His name and credit shall you undertake,
And in my house you shall be friendly lodged.
Look that you take upon you as you should,
110 You understand me, sir: so shall you stay
Till you have done your business in the city:

If this be court'sy, sir, accept of it.
Pedant. O, sir, I do, and will repute you ever
The patron of my life and liberty.
Tranio. Then go with me to make the matter good.
This, by the way, I let you understand—
My father is here looked for every day,
To pass assurance of a dower in marriage
'Twixt me and one Baptista's daughter here:
In all these circumstances I'll instruct you. 120
Go with me, sir, to clothe you as becomes you.
[*they go*

[4. 3.] *The hall of Petruchio's house in the country*

KATHARINA *and* GRUMIO

Grumio. No, no, forsooth, I dare not for my life
Katharina. The more my wrong, the more his spite appears.
What, did he marry me to famish me?
Beggars that come unto my father's door,
Upon entreaty have a present alms,
If not, elsewhere they meet with charity:
But I, who never knew how to entreat,
Nor never needed that I should entreat,
Am starved for meat, giddy for lack of sleep,
With oaths kept waking, and with brawling fed: 10
And that which spites me more than all these wants,
He does it under name of perfect love;
As who should say—if I should sleep or eat,
'Twere deadly sickness or else present death.
I prithee go, and get me some repast,
I care not what, so it be wholesome food.
Grumio. What say you to a neat's foot?
Katharina. 'Tis passing good, I prithee let me have it,

Grumio. I fear it is too choleric a meat.
20 How say you to a fat tripe finely broiled?
Katharina. I like it well. Good Grumio, fetch it me.
Grumio. I cannot tell, I fear 'tis choleric.
What say you to a piece of beef and mustard?
Katharina. A dish that I do love to feed upon.
Grumio. Ay, but the mustard is too hot a little.
Katharina. Why then, the beef, and let the mustard rest.
Grumio. Nay then, I will not, you shall have the mustard,
Or else you get no beef of Grumio.
Katharina. Then both or one, or any thing thou wilt.
30 *Grumio.* Why then, the mustard without the beef.
Katharina. Go, get thee gone, thou false deluding slave, [*she 'beats him'*
That feed'st me with the very name of meat.
Sorrow on thee and all the pack of you
That triumph thus upon my misery:
Go, get thee gone, I say.

'Enter PETRUCHIO *and* HORTENSIO *with meat'*

Petruchio. How fares my Kate? What, sweeting, all-amort?
Hortensio. Mistress, what cheer?
Katharina. Faith, as cold as can be.
Petruchio. Pluck up thy spirits, look cheerfully upon me.
Here, love, thou seest how diligent I am,
40 To dress thy meat myself, and bring it thee.
[*he sets the dish down; she falls to*
I am sure, sweet Kate, this kindness merits thanks.
[*she eats*
What, not a word? Nay then, thou lov'st it not;

And all my pains is sorted to no proof.
[*he snatches up the meat*
Here, take away this dish.
Katharina. I pray you, let it stand.
Petruchio. The poorest service is repaid with thanks,
And so shall mine before you touch the meat.
Katharina. I thank you, sir. [*he sets down the dish*
Hortensio. Signior Petruchio, fie! you are to blame:
Come, Mistress Kate, I'll bear you company.
[*he sits at the table*
(*Petruchio.* Eat it up all, Hortensio, if thou lovest me: 50
Much good do it unto thy gentle heart.
[*aloud*] Kate, eat apace; and now, my honey love,
Will we return unto thy father's house,
And revel it as bravely as the best,
With silken coats and caps and golden rings,
With ruffs and cuffs and fardingales, and things;
With scarfs and fans and double change of brav'ry,
With amber bracelets, beads, and all this knav'ry:
[*she looks up, and at a nod from him, Grumio swiftly removes the dishes*
What, hast thou dined? The tailor stays thy leisure,
To deck thy body with his ruffling treasure. 60

A tailor enters, with a gown upon his arm

Come, tailor, let us see these ornaments.
Lay forth the gown. [*the tailor spreads the gown upon the table; a haberdasher enters with a box*
What news with you, sir?
Haberdasher [*opens the box*]. Here is the cap your worship did bespeak.
Petruchio [*seizes it roughly*]. Why, this was moulded on a porringer—

A velvet dish: fie, fie! 'tis lewd and filthy:
Why, 'tis a cockle or a walnut-shell,
A knack, a toy, a trick, a baby's cap:
[*he casts it into a corner*
Away with it! come, let me have a bigger.
Katharina. I'll have no bigger, this doth fit the time,
70 And gentlewomen wear such caps as these.
Petruchio. When you are gentle, you shall have one too,
And not till then.
(*Hortensio.* That will not be in haste.
Katharina. Why, sir, I trust, I may have leave to speak,
And speak I will! I am no child, no babe—
Your betters have endured me say my mind,
And if you cannot, best you stop your ears.
My tongue will tell the anger of my heart,
Or else my heart concealing it will break,
And rather than it shall, I will be free,
80 Even to the uttermost, as I please, in words.
Petruchio. Why, thou say'st true—it is a paltry cap,
A custard-coffin, a bauble, a silken pie!
I love thee well, in that thou lik'st it not.
Katharina. Love me or love me not, I like the cap,
And it I will have, or I will have none.
Petruchio. Thy gown? why, ay: come, tailor, let us see't.
[*he goes to the table; Grumio dismisses the haberdasher*
O mercy, God! what masquing-stuff is here?
What's this? a sleeve? 'tis like a demi-cannon.
What! up and down carved like an apple-tart?
90 Here's snip and nip and cut and slish and slash,
Like to a censer in a barber's shop:
Why, what a devil's name, tailor, call'st thou this?
(*Hortensio.* I see she's like to have neither cap nor gown.

Tailor. You bid me make it orderly and well,
According to the fashion and the time.
Petruchio. Marry, and did; but if you be remembred,
I did not bid you mar it to the time.
Go, hop me over every kennel home,
For you shall hop without my custom, sir:
I'll none of it; hence, make your best of it. 100
Katharina. I never saw a better-fashioned gown,
More quaint, more pleasing, nor more commendable:
Belike you mean to make a puppet of me.
Petruchio. Why, true, he means to make a puppet
of thee.
Tailor. She says your worship means to make a puppet
of her.
Petruchio. O monstrous arrogance! Thou liest, thou
thread, thou thimble,
Thou yard, three-quarters, half-yard, quarter, nail!
Thou flea, thou nit, thou winter-cricket thou! 110
Braved in mine own house with a skein of thread?
Away, thou rag, thou quantity, thou remnant,
Or I shall so be-mete thee with thy yard,
As thou shalt think on prating whilst thou livest!
I tell thee, I, that thou hast marred her gown.
Tailor. Your worship is deceived—the gown is made
Just as my master had direction:
Grumio gave order how it should be done.
Grumio. I gave him no order, I gave him the stuff.
Tailor. But how did you desire it should be made? 120
Grumio. Marry, sir, with needle and thread.
Tailor. But did you not request to have it cut?
Grumio. Thou hast faced many things.
Tailor. I have.
Grumio. Face not me: thou hast braved many men,
brave not me; I will neither be faced nor braved. I say

unto thee, I bid thy master cut out the gown, but I did not bid him cut it to pieces: ergo, thou liest.

Tailor. Why, here is the note of the fashion to testify.

130 *Petruchio.* Read it.

Grumio. The note lies in's throat, if he say I said so.

Tailor [*reads*]. 'Imprimis, a loose-bodied gown.'

Grumio. Master, if ever I said loose-bodied gown, sew me in the skirts of it, and beat me to death with a bottom of brown thread: I said a gown.

Petruchio. Proceed.

Tailor. 'With a small compassed cape.'

Grumio. I confess the cape.

Tailor. 'With a trunk sleeve.'

140 *Grumio.* I confess two sleeves.

Tailor. 'The sleeves curiously cut.'

Petruchio. Ay, there's the villainy.

Grumio. Error i'th' bill, sir, error i'th' bill! I commanded the sleeves should be cut out, and sewed up again, and that I'll prove upon thee, though thy little finger be armed in a thimble.

Tailor. This is true that I say, an I had thee in place where, thou shouldst know it.

Grumio. I am for thee straight: take thou the bill, give
150 me thy mete-yard, and spare not me.

Hortensio. God-a-mercy, Grumio! then he shall have no odds.

Petruchio. Well, sir, in brief, the gown is not for me.

Grumio. You are i'th' right, sir, 'tis for my mistress.

Petruchio. Go, take it up unto thy master's use.

Grumio. Villain, not for thy life: take up my mistress' gown for thy master's use!

Petruchio. Why, sir, what's your conceit in that?

Grumio. O, sir, the conceit is deeper than you think for:
160 Take up my mistress' gown to his master's use!

O, fie, fie, fie!
(*Petruchio.* Hortensio, say thou wilt see the tailor paid.
[*aloud*] Go take it hence, be gone, and say no more.
(*Hortensio.* Tailor, I'll pay thee for thy gown to-morrow.
Take no unkindness of his hasty words:
Away, I say. Commend me to thy master.
[*the tailor goes*
Petruchio. Well, come my Kate, we will unto your father's,
Even in these honest mean habiliments:
Our purses shall be proud, our garments poor:
For 'tis the mind that makes the body rich, 170
And as the sun breaks through the darkest clouds,
So honour peereth in the meanest habit.
What, is the jay more precious than the lark,
Because his feathers are more beautiful?
Or is the adder better than the eel,
Because his painted skin contents the eye?
O, no, good Kate; neither art thou the worse
For this poor furniture, and mean array.
If thou account'st it shame, lay it on me.
And therefore frolic, we will hence forthwith, 180
To feast and sport us at thy father's house.
Go, call my men, and let us straight to him,
And bring our horses unto Long-lane end,
There will we mount, and thither walk on foot.
Let's see, I think 'tis now some seven o'clock,
And well we may come there by dinner-time.
Katharina. I dare assure you, sir, 'tis almost two,
And 'twill be supper-time ere you come there.
Petruchio. It shall be seven ere I go to horse:
Look, what I speak, or do, or think to do, 190
You are still crossing it. Sirs, let't alone,
I will not go to-day, and ere I do,

It shall be what o'clock I say it is.

Hortensio. Why, so this gallant will command the sun.

[*they go*

[4.4.] *The square in Padua*

TRANIO (*as Lucentio*) *with 'the Pedant, dressed like Vincentio', and 'booted' as newly arrived from a journey, draws near the house of Baptista*

Tranio. Sir, this is the house—please it you that I call?

Pedant. Ay, what else? and but I be deceived
Signior Baptista may remember me,
Near twenty years ago, in Genoa,
Where we were lodgers at the Pegasus.

Tranio. 'Tis well, and hold your own, in any case
With such austerity as 'longeth to a father.

Pedant. I warrant you.

BIONDELLO *approaches*

But, sir, here comes your boy.
'Twere good he were schooled.

10 *Tranio.* Fear you not him. Sirrah Biondello,
Now do your duty throughly, I advise you;
Imagine 'twere the right Vincentio.

Biondello. Tut, fear not me.

Tranio. But hast thou done thy ĕrrand to Baptista?

Biondello. I told him, that your father was at Venice,
And that you looked for him this day in Padua.

Tranio. Th'art a tall fellow; hold thee that to drink.

[*gives him money*

The door opens and BAPTISTA *comes out followed by* LUCENTIO, *as Cambio*

Here comes Baptista: set your countenance, sir.
Signior Baptista, you are happily met:

[*to the Pedant*] Sir, this is the gentleman I told you of. 20
I pray you, stand good father to me now,
Give me Bianca for my patrimony.
Pedant. Soft, son!
Sir, by your leave, having come to Padua
To gather in some debts, my son Lucentio
Made me acquainted with a weighty cause
Of love between your daughter and himself:
And for the good report I hear of you,
And for the love he beareth to your daughter,
And she to him, to stay him not too long, 30
I am content, in a good father's care,
To have him matched: and, if you please to like
No worse than I, upon some agreement
Me shall you find ready and willing
With one consent to have her so bestowed:
For curious I cannot be with you,
Signior Baptista, of whom I hear so well.
Baptista. Sir, pardon me in what I have to say—
Your plainness and your shortness please me well:
Right true it is, your son Lucentio here 40
Doth love my daughter, and she loveth him,
Or both dissemble deeply their affections:
And therefore, if you say no more than this,
That like a father you will deal with him,
And pass my daughter a sufficient dower,
The match is made, and all is done—
Your son shall have my daughter with consent.
Tranio. I thank you, sir. Where then do you know best
We be affied and such assurance ta'en
As shall with either part's agreement stand 50
Baptista. Not in my house, Lucentio, for you know
Pitchers have ears and I have many servants,

Besides, old Gremio is heark'ning still,
And happily we might be interrupted.
Tranio. Then at my lodging, an it like you.
There doth my father lie; and there this night
We'll pass the business privately and well:
Send for your daughter by your servant here,
[*he winks at Lucentio*
My boy shall fetch the scrivener presently.
60 The worst is this, that, at so slender warning,
You are like to have a thin and slender pittance.
Baptista. It likes me well: Cambio, hie you home,
And bid Bianca make her ready straight:
And, if you will, tell what hath happenéd—
Lucentio's father is arrived in Padua,
And how she's like to be Lucentio's wife.
[*Lucentio moves away, but at a privy sign from Tranio he stands by among the trees*
Biondello. I pray the gods she may, with all my heart!
Tranio. Dally not with the gods, but get thee gone.
[*he beckons him to join Lucentio*

A serving-man opens the door of Tranio's lodging

Signior Baptista, shall I lead the way?
70 Welcome! one mess is like to be your cheer.
Come sir, we will better it in Pisa.
Baptista. I follow you.
[*Tranio, Baptista and the Pedant go in; Lucentio and Biondello come forward*
Biondello. Cambio.
Lucentio. What say'st thou, Biondello?
Biondello. You saw my master wink and laugh upon you?
Lucentio. Biondello, what of that?

Biondello. Faith nothing; but has left me here behind, to expound the meaning or moral of his signs and tokens.

Lucentio. I pray thee, moralize them.

Biondello. Then thus...Baptista is safe, talking with the deceiving father of a deceitful son. 80

Lucentio. And what of him?

Biondello. His daughter is to be brought by you to the supper.

Lucentio. And then?

Biondello. The old priest at Saint Luke's church is at your command at all hours.

Lucentio. And what of all this?

Biondello. I cannot tell—except they are busied about a counterfeit assurance: take you assurance of her, 'cum privilegio ad imprimendum solum.' To th' church! 90 take the priest, clerk, and some sufficient honest witnesses.

If this be not that you look for, I have no more to say,
But bid Bianca farewell for ever and a day.

[*he turns to go*

Lucentio. Hear'st thou, Biondello?

Biondello. I cannot tarry: I knew a wench married in an afternoon as she went to the garden for parsley to stuff a rabbit—and so may you, sir; and so adieu, sir. My master hath appointed me to go to Saint Luke's, to bid the priest be ready to come against you come with 100 your appendix. [*he runs off*

Lucentio. I may and will, if she be so contented:
She will be pleased, then wherefore should I doubt?
Hap what hap may, I'll roundly go about her;
It shall go hard, if Cambio go without her. [*he goes*

[4. 5.] *A steep hill on the highway leading to Padua*

PETRUCHIO, KATHARINA, HORTENSIO and servants resting by the way

Petruchio [*rises*]. Come on, a God's name! once more toward our father's.
Good Lord, how bright and goodly shines the moon!
Katharina. The moon! the sun: it is not moonlight now.
Petruchio. I say it is the moon that shines so bright.
Katharina. I know it is the sun that shines so bright.
Petruchio. Now by my mother's son, and that's myself,
It shall be moon, or star, or what I list,
Or ere I journey to your father's house...
[*to the servants*] Go on, and fetch our horses back again—
10 Evermore crossed and crossed, nothing but crossed!
(*Hortensio.* Say as he says, or we shall never go.
Katharina. Forward, I pray, since we have come so far,
And be it moon, or sun, or what you please:
And if you please to call it a rush-candle,
Henceforth I vow it shall be so for me.
Petruchio. I say it is the moon.
Katharina. I know it is the moon.
Petruchio. Nay, then you lie: it is the blessèd sun.
Katharina. Then, God be blessed, it is the blessèd sun—
But sun it is not, when you say it is not,
20 And the moon changes even as your mind:
What you will have it named, even that it is,
And so it shall be still, for Katharine.
(*Hortensio.* Petruchio, go thy ways, the field is won.
Petruchio. Well, forward, forward! thus the bowl should run, [*he takes her arm*

And not unluckily against the bias.
But soft, what company is coming here?

VINCENTIO, in travelling dress, is seen coming behind them up the hill

[*to Vincentio*] Good morrow, gentle mistress, where away?
Tell me, sweet Kate, and tell me truly too,
Hast thou beheld a fresher gentlewoman?
Such war of white and red within her cheeks! 30
What stars do spangle heaven with such beauty,
As those two eyes become that heavenly face?
Fair lovely maid, once more good day to thee:
Sweet Kate, embrace her for her beauty's sake.

(*Hortensio*. A' will make the man mad, to make a woman of him.

Katharina. Young budding virgin, fair and fresh and sweet,
Whither away, or where is thy abode?
Happy the parents of so fair a child;
Happier the man, whom favourable stars 40
Allot thee for his lovely bed-fellow!

Petruchio. Why, how now, Kate! I hope thou art not mad.
This is a man, old, wrinkled, faded, withered,
And not a maiden, as thou say'st he is.

Katharina. Pardon, old father, my mistaking eyes,
That have been so bedazzled with the sun,
That every thing I look on seemeth green:
Now I perceive thou art a reverend father;
Pardon, I pray thee, for my mad mistaking.

Petruchio. Do, good old grandsire, and withal make known 50
Which way thou travellest—if along with us,

We shall be joyful of thy company.

Vincentio. Fair sir, and you my merry mistress,
That with your strange encounter much amazed me,
[*he bows*
My name is called Vincentio, my dwelling Pisa,
And bound I am to Padua, there to visit
A son of mine, which long I have not seen.

Petruchio. What is his name?

Vincentio. Lucentio, gentle sir.

Petruchio. Happily met—the happier for thy son.
60 And now by law, as well as reverend age,
I may entitle thee my loving father.
The sister to my wife, this gentlewoman,
Thy son by this hath married. Wonder not,
Nor be not grieved—she is of good esteem,
Her dowry wealthy, and of worthy birth;
Beside, so qualified as may beseem
The spouse of any noble gentleman.
Let me embrace with old Vincentio, [*they embrace*
And wander we to see thy honest son,
70 Who will of thy arrival be full joyous.

Vincentio. But is this true? or is it else your pleasure,
Like pleasant travellers, to break a jest
Upon the company you overtake?

Hortensio. I do assure thee, father, so it is.

Petruchio. Come, go along, and see the truth hereof,
For our first merriment hath made thee jealous.
[*they move on*

(*Hortensio.* Well, Petruchio, this hath put me in heart.
Have to my widow! and if she be froward,
Then hast thou taught Hortensio to be untoward.
[*he follows up the hill*

[5. 1.] *The square in Padua*

GREMIO seated under the trees, nodding; the door of Baptista's house opens softly; BIONDELLO, LUCENTIO (in his proper habit) and BIANCA (muffled) steal forth

Biondello [*whispers*]. Softly and swiftly, sir, for the priest is ready.

Lucentio. I fly, Biondello: but they may chance to need thee at home, therefore leave us.

[*he and Bianca pass swiftly from the square*

Biondello [*follows*]. Nay, faith, I'll see the church o'your back, and then come back to my master's as soon as I can.

Gremio [*rouses*]. I marvel Cambio comes not all this while.

'PETRUCHIO, KATHARINA, VINCENTIO, and GRUMIO with attendants' enter the square and approach the house where Tranio lodges

Petruchio. Sir, here's the door, this is Lucentio's house.
My father's bears more toward the market-place, 10
Thither must I, and here I leave you, sir.

Vincentio. You shall not choose but drink before you go;
I think I shall command your welcome here,
And by all likelihood some cheer is toward.

[*he 'knocks'*

Gremio [*comes forward*]. They're busy within, you were best knock louder. [*Petruchio raps soundly*

The 'Pedant looks out of the window' above the door

Pedant. What's he that knocks as he would beat down the gate?

Vincentio. Is Signior Lucentio within, sir?

20 *Pedant.* He's within, sir, but not to be spoken withal.

Vincentio. What if a man bring him a hundred pound or two, to make merry withal?

Pedant. Keep your hundred pounds to yourself, he shall need none, so long as I live.

Petruchio. Nay, I told you your son was well beloved in Padua...Do you hear, sir?—to leave frivolous circumstances, I pray you tell Signior Lucentio that his father is come from Pisa, and is here at the door to speak with him.

30 *Pedant.* Thou liest, his father is come from †Mantua, and is here looking out at the window.

Vincentio. Art thou his father?

Pedant. Ay, sir, so his mother says, if I may believe her.

Petruchio [*to Vincentio*]. Why, how now, gentleman! why, this is flat knavery, to take upon you another man's name.

Pedant. Lay hands on the villain! I believe, a' means to cozen somebody in this city under my countenance.

BIONDELLO returns

40 (*Biondello.* I have seen them in the church together, God send 'em good shipping. But who is here? mine old master Vincentio! now we are undone, and brought to nothing.

Vincentio [*sees Biondello*]. Come hither, crack-hemp.

Biondello [*passing by*]. I hope I may choose, sir.

Vincentio [*seizes him*]. Come hither, you rogue. What, have you forgot me?

Biondello. Forgot you? no, sir: I could not forget you, for I never saw you before in all my life.

50 *Vincentio.* What, you notorious villain, didst thou never see thy master's father, Vincentio?

Biondello. What, my old, worshipful old master? yes, marry, sir—see where he looks out of the window.

Vincentio. Is't so, indeed? [*'he beats Biondello'*

Biondello. Help, help, help! here's a madman will murder me. [*he runs away*

Pedant. Help, son! help, Signior Baptista!
[*he shuts the window*

Petruchio. Prithee, Kate, let's stand aside, and see the end of this controversy. [*they sit beneath the trees*

The 'Pedant with servants, BAPTISTA and TRANIO' come from the house, having sticks in their hands

Tranio. Sir, what are you, that offer to beat my servant? 60

Vincentio. What am I, sir! nay, what are you, sir? O immortal gods! O fine villain! A silken doublet, a velvet hose, a scarlet cloak, and a copatain hat! O, I am undone, I am undone! while I play the good husband at home, my son and my servant spend all at the university.

Tranio. How now! what's the matter?

Baptista. What, is the man lunatic?

Tranio. Sir, you seem a sober ancient gentleman by 70 your habit: but your words show you a madman. Why, sir, what 'cerns it you, if I wear pearl and gold? I thank my good father, I am able to maintain it.

Vincentio. Thy father! O, villain, he is a sail-maker in Bergamo.

Baptista. You mistake, sir—you mistake, sir—pray, what do you think is his name?

Vincentio. His name! as if I knew not his name: I have brought him up ever since he was three years old, and his name is Tranio. 80

Pedant. Away, away, mad ass! his name is Lucentio, and he is mine only son, and heir to the lands of me, Signior Vincentio.

Vincentio. Lucentio! O, he hath murdered his master! Lay hold on him, I charge you, in the duke's name. O, my son, my son...Tell me, thou villain, where is my son Lucentio?

Tranio. Call forth an officer.

An officer comes up

Carry this mad knave to the gaol. Father Baptista, I
90 charge you see that he be forthcoming.

Vincentio. Carry me to the gaol!

Gremio. Stay, officer. He shall not go to prison.

Baptista. Talk not, Signior Gremio; I say he shall go to prison.

Gremio. Take heed, Signior Baptista, lest you be cony-catched in this business; I dare swear this is the right Vincentio.

Pedant. Swear, if thou darest.

Gremio. Nay, I dare not swear it.

100 *Tranio.* Then thou wert best say that I am not Lucentio.

Gremio. Yes, I know thee to be Signior Lucentio.

Baptista. Away with the dotard, to the gaol with him!

Vincentio. Thus strangers may be haléd and abused. O monstrous villain!

BIONDELLO returns with LUCENTIO and BIANCA

Biondello. O, we are spoiled, and—yonder he is! Deny him, forswear him, or else we are all undone.

Lucentio [*'kneels'*]. Pardon, sweet father.

Vincentio. Lives my sweet son?

Biondello, Tranio, and Pedant run 'as fast as may be' into Lucentio's house

Bianca [*kneels*]. Pardon, dear father.
Baptista. How hast thou offended?
Where is Lucentio?
Lucentio. Here's Lucentio, 110
Right son to the right Vincentio,
That have by marriage made thy daughter mine,
While counterfeit supposes bleared thine eyne.
Gremio. Here's packing, with a witness, to deceive us all!
Vincentio. Where is that damnéd villain, Tranio,
That faced and braved me in this matter so?
Baptista. Why, tell me, is not this my Cambio?
Bianca. Cambio is changed into Lucentio.
Lucentio. Love wrought these miracles. Bianca's love 120
Made me exchange my state with Tranio,
While he did bear my countenance in the town,
And happily I have arrived at last
Unto the wishéd haven of my bliss.
What Tranio did, myself enforced him to;
Then pardon him, sweet father, for my sake.
Vincentio. I'll slit the villain's nose, that would have sent me to the gaol.
Baptista. But do you hear, sir? have you married my daughter without asking my good will? 130
Vincentio. Fear not, Baptista—we will content you, go to: but I will in, to be revenged for this villainy.
[*he forces open the door of Lucentio's house and goes within*
Baptista. And I, to sound the depth of this knavery.
[*he enters his own house*

Lucentio. Look not pale, Bianca; thy father will not frown. [*they follow Baptista*

Gremio. My cake is dough, but I'll in among the rest,
Out of hope of all but my share of the feast.
[*he follows likewise*

PETRUCHIO and KATHARINA rise

Katharina. Husband, let's follow, to see the end of this ado.

Petruchio. First kiss me, Kate, and we will.

Katharina. What, in the midst of the street?

140 *Petruchio.* What, art thou ashamed of me?

Katharina. No, sir, God forbid—but ashamed to kiss.

Petruchio. Why, then let's home again. [*to Grumio*] Come, sirrah, let's away.

Katharina. Nay, I will give thee a kiss. [*they kiss*] Now pray thee, love, stay.

Petruchio. Is not this well? Come, my sweet Kate.
Better once than never, for never too late.
[*they enter the house of Baptista, she leaning upon his arm*

[5. 2.] *A room in Lucentio's house*

Doors are opened by servants and there enter BAPTISTA and VINCENTIO, GREMIO and the Pedant, LUCENTIO and BIANCA, PETRUCHIO and KATHARINA, HORTENSIO and the Widow; 'the serving-men with TRANIO bringing in a banquet'

Lucentio. At last, though long, our jarring notes agree,
And time it is, when raging war is done,
To smile at scapes and perils overblown.
My fair Bianca, bid my father welcome,
While I with self-same kindness welcome thine:

Brother Petruchio, sister Katharina,
And thou, Hortensio, with thy loving widow,
Feast with the best, and welcome to my house.
My banquet is to close our stomachs up,
After our great good cheer. Pray you, sit down, 10
For now we sit to chat, as well as eat.
[*they sit; the servants proffer wine, fruit, and so forth*

Petruchio. Nothing but sit and sit, and eat and eat!

Baptista. Padua affords this kindness, son Petruchio.

Petruchio. Padua affords nothing but what is kind.

Hortensio. For both our sakes, I would that word were true.

Petruchio. Now, for my life, Hortensio fears his widow.

Widow. Then never trust me if I be afeard.

Petruchio. You are very sensible, and yet you miss my sense:
I mean, Hortensio is afeard of you.

Widow. He that is giddy thinks the world turns round. 20

Petruchio. Roundly replied.

Katharina. Mistress, how mean you that?

Widow. Thus I conceive by him.

Petruchio. Conceives by me! How likes Hortensio that?

Hortensio. My widow says, thus she conceives her tale.

Petruchio. Very well mended: kiss him for that, good widow.

Katharina. 'He that is giddy thinks the world turns round'—
I pray you, tell me what you meant by that.

Widow. Your husband, being troubled with a shrew,
Measures my husband's sorrow by his woe:
And now you know my meaning. 30

Katharina. A very mean meaning.

Widow. Right, I mean you.

Katharina. And I am mean, indeed, respecting you.
Petruchio. To her, Kate!
Hortensio. To her, widow!
Petruchio. A hundred marks, my Kate does put her down.
Hortensio. That's my office.
Petruchio. Spoke like an officer: ha' to thee, lad!
[*he 'drinks to Hortensio'*
Baptista. How likes Gremio these quick-witted folks?
Gremio. †Believe me, they butt heads together well.
40 *Bianca.* Head and butt! an hasty-witted body
Would say your head and butt were head and horn.
Vincentio. Ay, mistress bride, hath that awakened you?
Bianca. Ay, but not frighted me, therefore I'll sleep again.
Petruchio. Nay, that you shall not: since you have begun,
Have at you for a bitter jest or two.
Bianca. Am I your bird? I mean to shift my bush,
And then pursue me as you draw your bow.
You are welcome all.
[*she rises, curtsies to the company and leaves the chamber, followed by Katharina and the Widow*
Petruchio. She hath prevented me. Here, Signior Tranio,
50 This bird you aimed at, though you hit her not—
Therefore, a health to all that shot and missed.
Tranio. O, sir, Lucentio slipped me like his greyhound,
Which runs himself, and catches for his master.
Petruchio. A good swift simile, but something currish.
Tranio. 'Tis well, sir, that you hunted for yourself:
'Tis thought, your deer does hold you at a bay.
Baptista. O ho, Petruchio! Tranio hits you now.

Lucentio. I thank thee for that gird, good Tranio.
Hortensio. Confess, confess, hath he not hit you here?
Petruchio. A' has a little galled me, I confess; 60
And as the jest did glance away from me,
'Tis ten to one it maimed you two outright.
Baptista. Now, in good sadness, son Petruchio,
I think thou hast the veriest shrew of all.
Petruchio. Well, I say no: and therefore for assurance
Let's each one send unto his wife,
And he whose wife is most obedient,
To come at first when he doth send for her,
Shall win the wager which we will propose.
Hortensio. Content. What is the wager?
Lucentio. Twenty crowns. 70
Petruchio. Twenty crowns!
I'll venture so much of my hawk or hound,
But twenty times so much upon my wife.
Lucentio. A hundred then.
Hortensio. Content.
Petruchio. A match! 'tis done.
Hortensio. Who shall begin?
Lucentio. That will I.
Go, Biondello, bid your mistress come to me.
Biondello. I go. [*he goes*
Baptista. Son, I will be your half, Bianca comes.
Lucentio. I'll have no halves; I'll bear it all myself.

BIONDELLO *returns*

How now! what news?
Biondello. Sir, my mistress sends you word 80
That she is busy, and she cannot come.
Petruchio. How! she is busy, and she cannot come!
Is that an answer?
Gremio. Ay, and a kind one too:

Pray God, sir, your wife send you not a worse.
Petruchio. I hope better.
Hortensio. Sirrah Biondello, go and entreat my wife
To come to me forthwith. [*exit Biondello*
Petruchio. O, ho! entreat her!
Nay, then she must needs come.
Hortensio. I am afraid, sir,
Do what you can, yours will not be entreated...

BIONDELLO returns

90 Now, where's my wife?
Biondello. She says you have some goodly jest in hand.
She will not come; she bids you come to her.
Petruchio. Worse and worse, she will not come! O vile,
Intolerable, not to be endured!
Sirrah, Grumio, go to your mistress;
Say, I command her come to me. [*Grumio goes out*
Hortensio. I know her answer.
Petruchio. What?
Hortensio. She will not.
Petruchio. The fouler fortune mine, and there an end.

KATHARINA stands in the doorway

Baptista. Now, by my holidame, here comes Katharina!
100 *Katharina.* What is your will, sir, that you send for me?
Petruchio. Where is your sister, and Hortensio's wife?
Katharina. They sit conferring by the parlour fire.
Petruchio. Go, fetch them hither. If they deny to come,
Swinge me them soundly forth unto their husbands.
Away, I say, and bring them hither straight. [*she goes*
Lucentio. Here is a wonder, if you talk of wonders.

Hortensio. And so it is; I wonder what it bodes.
Petruchio. Marry, peace it bodes, and love, and quiet life,
An awful rule, and right supremacy;
And, to be short, what not, that's sweet and happy? 110
Baptista. Now fair befal thee, good Petruchio!
The wager thou hast won, and I will add
Unto their losses twenty thousand crowns—
Another dowry to another daughter,
For she is changed, as she had never been.
Petruchio. Nay, I will win my wager better yet,
And show more sign of her obedience,
Her new-built virtue and obedience.

KATHARINA returns with BIANCA and the Widow

See, where she comes, and brings your froward wives
As prisoners to her womanly persuasion. 120
Katharine, that cap of yours becomes you not,
Off with that bauble, throw it under-foot. [*she obeys*
Widow. Lord, let me never have a cause to sigh,
Till I be brought to such a silly pass!
Bianca. Fie! what a foolish duty call you this?
Lucentio. I would your duty were as foolish too:
The wisdom of your duty, fair Bianca,
Hath cost one hundred crowns since supper-time.
Bianca. The more fool you, for laying on my duty.
Petruchio. Katharine, I charge thee, tell these headstrong women 130
What duty they do owe their lords and husbands.
Widow. Come, come, you're mocking; we will have no telling.
Petruchio. Come on, I say, and first begin with her.
Widow. She shall not.
Petruchio. I say, she shall—and first begin with her.

Katharina. Fie, fie! unknit that threatening unkind brow,
And dart not scornful glances from those eyes,
To wound thy lord, thy king, thy governor:
It blots thy beauty as frosts do bite the meads,
140 Confounds thy fame as whirlwinds shake fair buds,
And in no sense is meet or amiable.
A woman moved is like a fountain troubled,
Muddy, ill-seeming, thick, bereft of beauty,
And while it is so, none so dry or thirsty
Will deign to sip or touch one drop of it.
Thy husband is thy lord, thy life, thy keeper,
Thy head, thy sovereign; one that cares for thee,
And for thy maintenance commits his body
To painful labour, both by sea and land;
150 To watch the night in storms, the day in cold,
Whilst thou liest warm at home, secure and safe,
And craves no other tribute at thy hands,
But love, fair looks, and true obedience;
Too little payment for so great a debt.
Such duty as the subject owes the prince,
Even such a woman oweth to her husband:
And when she is froward, peevish, sullen, sour,
And not obedient to his honest will,
What is she but a foul contending rebel,
160 And graceless traitor to her loving lord?
I am ashamed that women are so simple
To offer war where they should kneel for peace;
Or seek for rule, supremacy, and sway,
When they are bound to serve, love, and obey.
Why are our bodies soft, and weak, and smooth,
Unapt to toil and trouble in the world,
But that our soft conditions and our hearts
Should well agree with our external parts?

Come, come, you froward and unable worms!
My mind hath been as big as one of yours, 170
My heart as great, my reason haply more,
To bandy word for word, and frown for frown;
But now I see our lances are but straws,
Our strength as weak, our weakness past compare,
That seeming to be most which we indeed least are.
Then vail your stomachs, for it is no boot,
And place your hands below your husband's foot:
In token of which duty, if he please,
My hand is ready, may it do him ease.

Petruchio. Why, there's a wench! Come on, and kiss me, Kate. 180

Lucentio. Well, go thy ways, old lad, for thou shalt ha't.

Vincentio. 'Tis a good hearing, when children are toward.

Lucentio. But a harsh hearing when women are froward.

Petruchio. Come Kate, we'll to bed.
We three are married, but you two are sped.
'Twas I won the wager, though you hit the white,
[*to Lucentio*
And, being a winner, God give you good night!
[*Petruchio and Katharina depart*

Hortensio. Now go thy ways, thou hast tamed a curst shrow.

Lucentio. 'Tis a wonder, by your leave, she will be taméd so. [*they all go off to bed*

THE COPY FOR
THE TAMING OF THE SHREW, 1623

The First Folio provides us with the sole primary text of the play in this volume, and though we shall, at a later stage of our enquiry, have to glance for a moment or two at a curious version published in 1594, that version possesses no textual authority whatever, and the modern editor has therefore to be content with what was printed in 1623. Unfortunately it is far from being one of the best of the Folio texts, though its numerous imperfections are individually for the most part trivial in character.

A. *The nature of the Copy*

(i) *The omission or addition of small words.* Its most obvious and, to an editor, its most irritating feature is the presence of a number of lines which have been metrically ruined by the omission, or less often by the addition, of some small word or words. Apart from short lines some of which appear to be due to revision or adaptation, we have counted over forty of these metrically imperfect lines. When the defect has impaired sense as well as metre editors have been generally forced to emend, and it will illustrate the character of the textual malady if we here give a list of such emended verse-lines as have been accepted by the editors of the *Globe Shakespeare*:

Will't please your lord*ship* drink a cup of sack	Ind. ii. 2.
And her withholds from me *and* other more	1. 2. 119.
Of all thy suitors, here I charge *thee*, tell	2. 1. 8.
Much more a shrew of *thy* impatient humour	3. 2. 29.
As *I* before imparted to your worship	3. 2. 128.
Why, thou say'st true—it is *a* paltry cap	4. 3. 81.
What's this? a sleeve? 'tis like *a* demi-cannon	4. 3. 88.
Have to my widow! and if she *be* froward	4. 5. 78.

Where the metre alone is affected, conservative editors have been naturally more chary in accepting emendation, though the offers have been plentiful enough; and one reason for their hesitation is that, as often as not, there are at least two possible alternatives for filling up the line. An interesting point about the business is that some parts of the text seem to be far more seriously corrupted than others. Thus 2. 1., though a long scene of over 400 lines, is hardly affected at all, while 3. 2., which is under 260, contains about a quarter of our total number of imperfect lines for the whole play. Moreover, in 3. 2., as occasionally elsewhere in the text, the corrupt lines seem to crowd upon each other. And one of the examples just quoted from this scene is followed by a short prose speech by Biondello from which, as appears from Baptista's reply, the word 'old' has been omitted, thus proving that the corrupting agency, whatever it was, did not restrict its operation to verse (v. note 3. 2. 30).

Now compositors are, of course, prone to little omissions or additions of this kind; and, as a matter of fact, in the F. text of *Much Ado*, of which we can check the misprints with assurance, since it was reprinted from the extant quarto of 1600, we found about the same number of verbal omissions and additions as occur in *The Shrew*[1]. The comparison, however, is not altogether a fair one to the printers of the Folio; for the prose passages which *The Shrew* contains—about 480 lines—may conceal much undetected corruption, seeing that far the larger proportion of the verbal omissions and additions in F. *Much Ado* make no perceptible difference to the sense and would have passed absolutely unnoticed had we not possessed the 1600 quarto for collation. It is safer, therefore, in every way to take as our standard of comparison some text which, like

[1] v. *Ado*, pp. 154–5.

The Shrew itself, is mainly in verse. *A Midsummer-Night's Dream* will serve well enough. The F. text of this play was printed from the Jaggard Quarto of 1619, and in the course of the reprinting the F. compositors added no more than ten misprints of the type we are considering. It would seem then that the number of misprints in *The Shrew* is quite abnormal for a verse-play, and would be abnormal even if we omitted 3. 2. with its particularly heavy crop of errors. Of course the explanation of this abnormality may lie in Jaggard's office: the master-printer perhaps found it necessary to entrust the text of *The Shrew* to an unusually incompetent couple of compositors. On the other hand, it is equally probable that the trouble sprang from the copy itself, and, if so, it must be attributed to careless transcription.

(ii) *Elaborate stage-directions, and auditory misprints.* If in respect to the corruption just noticed the F. text of *The Shrew* reminds us of *Measure for Measure*[1], in other points it bears a strong resemblance to that of *Errors*. This affinity is perhaps most striking in regard to the stage-directions, which are not merely quite unusually elaborate in both texts, but are framed on the same principles and, as we shall see, were perhaps written by the same hand. It is true that *The Shrew* contains none of those locality-directions which we found so interesting in *Errors*[2], probably because never more than two 'houses' are needed at one time on the stage; but it provides locality-directions of another kind which are no less interesting, e.g. the well-known 'Pedant lookes out of the window' (5. 1. 16), and the more remarkable and, we think, hitherto unnoticed 'Enter Biondello, Lucentio and Bianca, Gremio is out before' (5. 1. head)[3]. It contains too a plentiful supply

[1] *Measure*, pp. 109–10. [2] *Errors*, pp. 71–4.

[3] Sir Edmund Chambers, as far as we can discover, does not refer to it in his *Elizabethan Stage*.

of property-directions, such as 'Tranio, with his boy bearing a Lute and Bookes' (2. 1. 38), 'Enter one with water' (4. 1. 139); of costume-directions, such as 'Enter Tranio braue' (1. 2. 215), 'Lucentio, in the habit of a meane man' (2. 1. 38), 'the Pedant dreſt like Vincentio' (4. 4. head); and of action-directions such as 'Lucen. Tranio, ſtand by' (1. 1. 45), 'They ſit and marke' (1. 1. 252), 'He rings him by the eares' (1. 2. 17), 'Flies after Bianca' (2. 1. 29), and many others. All these are exactly in the manner of the directions in *Errors*. But beyond this general resemblance, we have in two instances a verbal similarity which, in our view, goes some way towards establishing identity of authorship for these stage-directions. The parallels are as follows: (i) *Errors*, 5. 1. 129 'Enter the Duke of Ephesus, and the Merchant of Siracuse bare head, with the Headsman, & other Officers,' and *Shrew*, 4. 4. 17 'Enter Baptista and Lucentio: Pedant booted and bare headed'; (ii) *Errors*, 4. 4. 145 'Exeunt omnes, as fast as may be, frighted,' and *Shrew*, 5. 1. 108 'Exit Biondello, Tranio and Pedant as faſt as may be.' Standing by itself, the occurrence of 'bare headed' in the stage-directions of both plays might be regarded as a coincidence[1], but taking it in conjunction with the striking duplication of the phrase 'as fast as may be' we find it hard to resist the impression that the directions in *The Shrew* may have been penned by the hand responsible for those of *Errors*, the hand which in our textual analysis of that play we described as Hand B to distinguish it from the different Hand A which wrote the dialogue.

If this be provisionally entertained as at least a possibility, further questions arise. Were the two texts pre-

[1] Dr Greg points out that the term occurs in an imperfectly preserved playhouse-plot which he identifies with that of *Fortune's Tennis* (? by Dekker for the Admiral's Company in 1600); v. *Henslowe Papers*, pp. 143-44.

pared at the same date and for the same occasion? And was the process of preparation similar in both instances? On the last point, there is evidence that, as with the text of *Errors*, dictation entered into the process of transmission of *The Shrew*, and there is even a likelihood that if Hand B had a share in the latter it was limited as in the former to the addition of the directions. That the directions were inserted by a different hand from that responsible for the dialogue is suggested by a number of clues such as the fact that while the name 'Tranio' is always spelt correctly in the dialogue, it sometimes appears as 'Trayno' or even 'Triano' in the stage-directions. A clue of another kind is furnished by two passages in which the speech-headings for Hortensio and Lucentio have become confused, while in one of the two the name Bianca is likewise involved. In quoting these passages from the F., we mark the correct distribution by printing bracketed speech-headings on the left of the dialogue.

(*a*) 4. 2. 1–8:

Enter Tranio and Hortenſio:

[*Tra.*] *Tra.* Is't poſsible friend *Liſio*, that miſtris *Bianca*
Doth fancie any other but *Lucentio*,
I tel you ſir, ſhe beares me faire in hand.
[*Hort.*] *Luc.* Sir, to ſatisfie you in what I haue ſaid,
Stand by, and marke the manner of his teaching.

Enter Bianca.

[*Luc.*] *Hor.* Now Miſtris, profit you in what you reade?
[*Bian.*] *Bian.* What Maſter reade you firſt, reſolue me that?
[*Luc.*] *Hor.* I reade, that I profeſſe the Art to loue.

(*b*) 3. 1. 46–60:

[*Hort.*] *Hort.* Madam, tis now in tune.
[*Luc.*] *Luc.* All but the baſe.
[*Hort.*] *Hort.* The baſe is right, 'tis the baſe knaue that iars.

Luc. How fiery and forward our Pedant is,
Now for my life the knaue doth court my loue,
Pedaſcule, Ile watch you better yet:
[*Bian.*] In time I may beleeue, yet I miſtruſt.
[*Luc.*] *Bian.* Miſtruſt it not, for ſure *Æacides*
Was *Aiax* cald ſo from his grandfather.
[*Bian.*] *Hort.* I muſt beleeue my maſter, elſe I promiſe you,
I ſhould be arguing ſtill vpon that doubt,
But let it reſt, now *Litio* to you:
Good maſter take it not vnkindly pray
That I haue beene thus pleaſant with you both.
[*Hort.*] *Hort.* You may go walk, and giue me leaue a while,
My Leſſons make no muſicke in three parts.

It seems a pretty imbroglio; yet the explanation, if we mistake not, is simple enough. Hortensio's dramatic pseudonym is Licio; he is addressed as such in the two scenes from which our passages are taken, and the name carried with it a costume-disguise, that of a music-master. For stage-purposes, therefore, Licio would be as good a label as Hortensio, and there is no difficulty in supposing that in the disguise scenes it was used in the acting-copy or the player's part to distinguish Hortensio's speeches. And, if so, the source of the textual corruption is revealed; for nothing could be easier than to mistake *Lic.* for *Luc.*, while if the speech-headings were written with minuscule initials, as was so frequently the case in Elizabethan playhouse manuscript, we can see how the name Bianca was dragged in as well, inasmuch as *li.*, *lu.* and *bi.*, or even *lic.*, *luc.* and *bia.*, might look very similar in careless English script.

But if this be the true explanation, it presupposes editorial interference of some kind with the text, since it is not to be supposed that any compositor would take it upon him to effect the changes which have given us the passages as they stand in the Folio. Moreover, it is clear that these changes had been carried out either by the person whom we have identified with Hand B of *Errors* or before that person began to work upon the text, for the simple reason that the confusion has in the first of the two passages affected the stage-directions. That at 4. 2. 5 ought of course to read 'Enter Bianca and Lucentio,' but faced by the speech-heading 'Luc.' in l. 4 the framer of the direction has been compelled to drop the second name. In a word, the F. text seems to have been printed from some kind of transcript, the dialogue and the stage-directions being the products of two distinct processes, and probably of two different hands.

Nevertheless the scribe responsible for the dialogue was clearly not the careful transcriber and normal speller whom we called Hand A in *Errors*. The numerous though trivial omissions and additions noted in section (i) above, if we are to lay them at his door, point to a constitutional inaccuracy, while his spelling, unlike that of Hand A, has nothing suggestive of the printing-house. Yet it seems likely that he took down his lines from dictation in the same fashion as the transcriber of *Errors*. Apart from the omissions and additions just referred to, *The Shrew* is on the whole a tolerably clean text, and it does not contain many misprints of the substitution type. Now of these quite a large proportion may be attributed to an error of the ear and not to one of the eye. For example 'goods' for 'gauds' (2. 1. 3), 'bots Waid' for 'bots swayed' (3. 2. 54), 'But ſir' for 'But to her' (3. 2. 126), 'come' for 'done' (5. 2. 2), and 'too' twice for 'two' (5. 2. 45, 62) all seem more likely to be mishearings than misprints. And though the amusing transmutation of 'Marseilles' to 'Marcellus' (2. 1. 368) might be explained as a not impossible misprint[1], the F2 reading 'Marsellis' gives us the contemporary English pronunciation of the French name and shows us how

[1] If we suppose that the spelling 'Marcellis' stood in the copy.

easily the ear might mistake it for the Roman cognomen. In short *The Shrew* and *Errors* belong to the same species of text, a species of which the characteristic marks are transcription (probably from dictation) and elaborate stage-directions after the fashion of Hand B.

(iii) *Acting company*. In discussing the text of *Errors* we reached the provisional theory that Hand B was an actor of some kind and that his work upon that play belonged to the early 'nineties, our ground being that the strange titles 'Antipholis Erotes' and 'Antipholis Sereptus' which he bestows upon Antipholus of Syracuse and Antipholus of Ephesus, indicate his familiarity with a play intermediate in development between the *Menæchmi* of Plautus and the *Errors* of Shakespeare, possibly the old *Historie of Error*. The discovery of his presence in *The Shrew* would enable us to date his activities with more precision and to associate them with a definite acting company.

Four plays in the Shakespeare canon have been generally regarded as having come to him from, or been written by him for, a mysterious and apparently short-lived company known as the Earl of Pembroke's men, of whom nothing is heard before 1592, who played twice at Court in the winter of 1592–3, and who were either bankrupt or near to it by September 1593. These plays are *The Taming of the Shrew*, *Titus Andronicus*, and 2 and 3 *Henry VI*, and the supposition rests on the fact that versions of all four plays, together with the text of Marlowe's *Edward II*, appeared from the press during the period 1593–4, with the name of the Earl of Pembroke's men on their title-pages[1]. The said texts, however, are of varying quality;

[1] As a matter of fact *The First Part of the Contention*, as the quarto version of 2 *Henry VI* is entitled, was not actually ascribed to the Pembroke men; but since its sequel *The True Tragedie* belonged to them we need not hesitate to believe *The First Part* did also.

for while *Edward II* is a good text and *Titus Andronicus*, save for the omission of one short scene, identical with the play as printed in the First Folio, the other three, viz. *The Taming of a Shrew*, *The first part of the Contention betwixt the two famous houses of Yorke and Lancaster*, and *The true tragedie of Richard Duke of Yorke and the death of good King Henrie the Sixt*—to give them their quarto titles—are very inferior to the corresponding versions first printed in 1623. Until quite recently this inferiority was accounted for on the theory that they were either Shakespeare's 'first drafts' made for the Pembroke company or 'old plays' which came into the hands of the Chamberlain's men from Pembroke's company, when the latter got into low water, and were subsequently revised by Shakespeare. Within the last four years, however, the position has entirely changed. In 1923 Dr W. W. Greg published his *Alcazar and Orlando* in which by a minute analysis of the extant text of Greene's *Orlando Furioso*, a quarto printed in 1594 like those just referred to, he demonstrated that it was possible for the members of an acting company, forced by poverty or bankruptcy into selling the prompt-copy of a play, to vamp up some kind of reconstructed text from their combined memories of the original. Thus was established the existence of a new and hitherto unsuspected type of Bad Quarto, the text transmitted wholesale by reporting, and thus Dr Greg succeeded in laying one more foundation stone in the edifice of Elizabethan scholarship. The first to build upon it was Mr Peter Alexander, who in three articles printed by the editor of *The Times Literary Supplement* (Oct. 9, Nov. 27, 1924; and Sept. 16, 1926) proved conclusively in my opinion[1] that *The First Part of the Contention*, *The True Tragedie*, and lastly *The Taming*

[1] A conviction my co-editor does altogether not share. v. pp. xiii–xiv, xxiii–xxiv. (D.W.)

of a Shrew were all 'reported texts' of this kind, and so far from being prior to the Folio versions were in point of fact demonstrably memorised reproductions of them. What this means as regards Shakespeare's handling of the play which belongs to this volume we shall examine in a moment.

The story, as far as external evidence goes, is completed by certain entries in Henslowe's *Diary* which show the Chamberlain's men, of which Shakespeare was a member at Christmas, 1594, if not earlier, acting for ten days at the beginning of June that year with the Admiral's men, and including among their performances one of 'the tamynge of A Shrowe.' This entry, hitherto taken as a reference to the spurious *A Shrew* printed in 1594, is now seen to be the first recorded (though assuredly not the earliest) performance of Shakespeare's *The Shrew*. 'Presumably,' pursues Mr Alexander, 'Pembroke's men were forced by circumstances to sell their interest' in this as well as other texts. 'A remnant of the company, however, although deprived of their former books, may have made a further visit to the provinces with such makeshift productions as *The Contention* and *A Shrew*,' which they were later forced to sell in their turn to the publishers in 1594. To this we may add that, as *The Contention* was entered in the Stationers' Register on March 12, 1594, and *A Shrew* on May 2 of the same year it is likely that if the Pembroke men possessed better texts of these plays they had handed them on to the Strange's, later the Chamberlain's, men when they themselves returned from the country in a bankrupt condition during July or August 1593, possibly even as early as July 6, when *Edward II* was entered in the Stationers' Register, especially as *Titus Andronicus* seems from its title-page to have passed from the Pembroke men to the Sussex men before it was entered in the Register on Feb. 6, 1594. And yet it is at least doubtful whether it is right to speak, as

Mr Alexander does, of the Pembroke men 'selling' copy to the Strange men, seeing that, if Sir Edmund Chambers is correct, the Pembroke company of 1592–3 was not independent of and rival to the Strange-Chamberlain men, but merely a temporary amalgamation, for the purpose of provincial touring, of certain members of the latter company together with certain members of the Admiral's men. A touring company of this kind would of course require acting copy; but it is most unlikely considering the risks of the road in those days that they would carry original prompt-copies about with them. In a word, they would have to be furnished with transcripts of some sort.

Whether the travelling company would acquire full rights over secondary dramatic texts of this kind is a matter for speculation. On general grounds it would seem natural that the principal men, who would probably be sharers in the parent company, would see to it that the manuscripts returned with them. That this did not happen in the case of *Edward II* and *Titus Andronicus* may be explained by the desperate financial straits in which Pembroke's men found themselves in the summer of 1593. We know that they had to pawn their costumes[1]; there would therefore be a strong temptation to raise money on the prompt-books. Nor need we suppose that the two texts were disposed of without the consent of the Strange's men, who were themselves probably in low water at this date. Some years later when they had become the Chamberlain's men, they were ready enough to release to the printers prompt-copies of Shakespearian plays the stage-popularity of which was at the ebb. Moreover, if they allowed the Pembroke men to make money by disposing of their transcripts, the originals almost certainly remained in their own hands. We can be tolerably certain of this as regards

[1] Greg, *Henslowe Papers*, p. 40.

Titus Andronicus, inasmuch as the Folio version of that play, though set up from a reprint of the 1594 quarto, contains a scene never before printed, which must have been derived from a second and presumably better text at the Globe. No second text of *Edward II* has survived to provide us with evidence. Nevertheless, there are one or two points about the text of 1594 which suggest that it was printed from a playhouse transcript.

In any event, we have in *Titus Andronicus* and *Edward II* two good (though not perfect) texts printed in 1593–4, with the name of Pembroke's company on their title-pages, and in *The Shrew* and the second and third parts of *Henry VI* three good (though also probably not 'original') texts, of which inferior versions, printed 1594–5, were ascribed to the same company, while all five texts, together with that of *Errors*, to say nothing of other F. plays yet to be dealt with, are clearly seen to belong to one playhouse family, their stage-directions in particular coming from the same mint. Is it a very wild hypothesis that in these half-dozen or so texts we have a body of Pembroke men's plays and that Hand B was the book-holder or stage-manager of the temporary company? The fact that the name of the company appears on the title-pages of garbled versions in the case of three texts does not prove that better texts could not have belonged to it. On the contrary, the ascription of such inferior dramatic material to reputable companies who were known to have acted in the authentic plays was one of the commonest dodges of shady Elizabethan printers who dealt in playhouse copy.

And yet, unless we are very much mistaken, these garbled texts were not altogether without cause connected with the name of the Earl of Pembroke's company. How, for example, are we to account for that degradation of *The Shrew* of which the text of *A Shrew* is witness? Mr Alexander, as we have seen, believes that *A Shrew* was vamped up by 'a remnant of the company,' who 'deprived of their former books' were forced to seek a living by making a further visit into the provinces relying upon their memories alone. Speaking generally, we think this the most probable explanation. But the texts of *A Shrew*, *The First Part of the Contention*, and *The True Tragedie of Richard Duke of Yorke* do not stand alone; for, as Mr Dugdale Sykes has convinced most of his readers, the first at any rate is linked by certain unmistakable stylistic marks not only with other 1594 texts such as *Orlando Furioso* and *The Famous Victories of Henry the fifth*, but also with plays published at a much later date such as *Doctor Faustus*, 1616, and *Wily Beguiled*, 1606[1]. It may be added in passing that one of the tricks of which Mr Sykes makes most successful use in his investigation —the exclamation 'sounes'—occurs several times in *The Contention*[2], a fact that still further links the degenerate *Henry VI* plays with the equally degenerate *Shrew* play. In short, while *The Shrew* is connected by its stage-directions with one group of plays, *A Shrew* belongs to yet another family of playhouse texts, of which *Orlando Furioso* is a typical example. And this second group are debased versions of what were originally good plays, reconstructed by some company which, having lost its prompt-books, was forced to fall back upon its collective memory eked out by one writer, or possibly two, of very indifferent dramatic powers. That is to say the textual degradation was a reflection of a deterioration in the company concerned.

At Christmas 1592 we find the Pembroke men achieving that pinnacle of a company's ambition, performance at Court; by July or August 1593 they were bankrupt, selling texts like *Edward II* to the stationers

[1] H. Dugdale Sykes, *Sidelights on Elizabethan Drama*, pp. 49–78.

[2] E.g. on pp. 50, 51, 55 of the Griggs facsimile.

and probably at the same time *Titus Andronicus* to the Sussex men, and even forced to pawn their costumes. Yet *A Shrew*, *Orlando Furioso*, *The Famous Victories*, and *The First Part of the Contention* did not get into print until the following spring, the first three named being all significantly entered in the Stationers' Register during the month of May. It is natural to suppose that these texts originated in the winter of 1593–4, and that a 'remnant' of the original Pembroke men had something to do with their creation. It is however exceedingly unlikely, we think, that Pembroke men alone were concerned. It will be accepted as a truism that reconstructed texts of the kind we are dealing with, however much they may owe to the invention of play-house scribes, a debt that is very clear for example in the case of *A Shrew*, must ultimately be derived from the memories of actors who have played in the original versions. But if this be so, we may well ask what *Orlando Furioso* for example is doing in this galley. It is a play the original of which is known for certain to have been acted by the company of which Edward Alleyn was the leader, for Alleyn's part in the title-rôle has survived to this day. It is also known for certain that Alleyn had nothing to do with the Pembroke company, since while they were on tour in 1593, he himself was travelling with another troupe of players who called themselves the Strange's men. It is plausible to suppose, therefore, that the bookless company who went on tour during the winter of 1593–4 and were responsible for the vamped-up plays we are considering, included a 'remnant' also of Alleyn's former fellow-actors. Indeed, if it be legitimate to estimate the size or quality of the contingent from the comparative goodness of the text, the Strange men remnant may have been stronger than the Pembroke men remnant inasmuch as the text of *Orlando* is certainly far closer to the original than is that of *A Shrew*. Moreover, there is yet a third company to reckon with—the Queen's men, whose name appears on the title-page of *The Famous Victories*, and who are known to have possessed the old Prince Hal plays from which that strangely distorted production was derived. *The Famous Victories*, however, the crudest of all these reconstructed texts, is so poor a thing that the memories upon which it was based may well have been some years old. That is to say the actors responsible for it may have been Pembroke or Strange men who had formerly been members of the Queen's company.

The salient fact which underlies all these obscure happenings in the theatrical world is the outbreak and continuance during 1592–4 of the worst plague of Elizabeth's reign. According to Sir Edmund Chambers, early in 1592 a 'large London company formed by the amalgamation of Strange's and the Admiral's[1]' under the leadership of Edward Alleyn, was playing at Henslowe's theatre, the Rose. In July the London theatres were closed on account of the plague, and Alleyn's combine, far too large for a travelling company, was forced reluctantly into 'division and separacion,' a division that is into two separate touring companies. One of these can be traced in an official document of 6 May 1593 as consisting of Alleyn, William Kempe, Thomas Pope, John Heminge, Augustine Phillips, and George Bryan, while it appears that Richard Cowley and Thomas Downton joined that troupe at a subsequent date[2]. This company travelled under the name of my Lord Strange's men. The other company, according to Sir Edmund Chambers' plausible conjecture, was that styling itself the Earl of Pembroke's. We have no information about its personnel, though as the name of Richard Burbage is absent from the list of Alleyn's fellows, it would not

[1] *Eliz. Stage*, ii. 129. [2] *Ibid.* ii. 123–4.

be surprising if he were the leader of this second company. It is at any rate certain that the company was a reputable one, since it was playing, as we have seen, at Court during the Christmas festivities 1592–3. The plague slackened somewhat at this period and there was actually a short season at the Rose, beginning Dec. 29, 1592. But on Jan. 28 the Privy Council once again issued an order closing all London playhouses, and the two companies after perhaps waiting about for a period in hope of abatement were no doubt forced to take to the road once more. London companies only turned to the provinces as a last resort, and it is probable that the continuance of the plague made the strolling player less and less acceptable as time went on to the dignitaries of country towns. In any case the Pembroke men in the summer of 1593 were, as we have seen, already at the end of their resources; and it may be supposed that Alleyn's company though keeping its head above water was none too happy at a prospect of indefinite banishment from the capital. We know nothing of what happened in the winter of 1593–4. And it is surely remarkable that neither the Pembroke nor the Strange men acted at Court, though the recorded appearance of the Queen's men shows that there was no cessation of Court performances on account of the plague.

Two things, however, may be said. At a time of severe stress, such as the evidence points to, the first step that the 'sharers' would feel forced to take would be to free themselves from their financial obligations to the hired men and boys in their employment. Some necessity of this nature may well account for the existence of the debased texts we have just been reviewing. We suggest, in short, that the company responsible for these texts was mostly composed of hired men and boys, formerly attached to the Pembroke and Strange companies, and perhaps led by Samuel Rowley, whose hand Mr Sykes believes he has found in most of the said texts. And the second thing to be said is that the correlative of such a company, viz. a small but strong troupe consisting almost entirely of sharers, may have sought employment far from London at the house of some great nobleman. We have found reason for thinking that Shakespeare was busy on the first draft of *As You Like It* in the summer of 1593, on the first draft of *Love's Labour's Lost* a few months later, and on the first draft of *The Merchant of Venice* early in 1594[1]. For what company was he working, if not for that which, including Richard Burbage and William Kempe, was performing at Court as the Lord Chamberlain's company in the winter of 1594–5? These plays, however, were not being prepared for the Court, since as we have just noted none but the Queen's men played before Her Majesty in the winter of 1593–4. 'Shakespeare's first handling of *Love's Labour's Lost*,' we wrote in our textual note upon that play, 'was clearly in preparation for some performance at Christmas, 1593. This performance was almost certainly a private and not a public one, both because the play was caviare to the general and because all the public playhouses... were closed on account of the plague. As we have already suggested, it was probably given at the house of the Earl of Southampton[2].'

(iv) *Actors' names in 'The Shrew' and other Pembroke men texts.* We have seen in previous volumes of this edition that actors' names, either in full or contracted form, are liable occasionally to crop up in the speech-headings and stage-directions of playhouse copy, the appearance of Kempe and Cowley in the text of *Much Ado*, 4. 2. being a famous example[3]. It so happens that

[1] v. *A.Y.L.* pp. 107–8; *L.L.L.* pp. 126–7; *M.V.* pp. 115–9.

[2] *L.L.L.* p. 127.

[3] See *Actors' names in basic Shakespearian texts* by Allison Gaw (Pub. Mod. Lang. Ass. America, Sept. 1925) for a general discussion of the phenomenon.

the F. texts of *The Shrew* and 2 and 3 *Henry VI* are unusually rich in these actors' names. It is true that for the most part they belong to minor players, and are sometimes merely abbreviated Christian names, yet taken as a whole they are worthy of consideration as providing clues which ought at least to prove serviceable to future investigators. We should like to be able to think that they throw light upon the personnel of the Pembroke company for which, as we have seen, the plays were probably prepared. Unfortunately, however, playhouse copy which was not published until 1623 was subject to all sorts of possible changes during the thirty years that had elapsed since 1593. Nevertheless, we have found no trace of such changes, unless it be the reference to Soto, which was conceivably, though not in our judgment probably, inserted after Shakespeare's death (v. note, Ind. i. 87).

We shall attempt therefore to bring out the facts, on the assumption that they may bear upon the composition of the Pembroke men, without however venturing to build too much upon them.

The third part of *Henry VI*, as has long been recognised, contains the names of three actors, viz. Sincklo and the Christian names Gabriel and Humfrey, which last belong with small doubt to Gabriel Spencer and Humphrey Jeffes, of whom we know little but who were both acting for a second Pembroke's company which was performing in 1597 and, when that collapsed like its predecessor, joined the Admiral's men in October of the same year. Of Sincklo or Sincler even less is known; but as his name appears in the plot of 2 *Seven Deadly Sins*, which was being played by either the Strange's or the Admiral's or the conjoint company about 1590 to 1592, in 3 *Henry VI* (3. 1. 1), *The Shrew* (Ind. i. 87), the 1600 quarto of 2 *Henry IV* (5. 4. 1), and the Induction to Marston's *Malecontent* (1604), it is a fairly safe inference that he was a small part actor who belonged first to Strange's or the Admiral's and was later a member of the Chamberlain's company. Still more obscure is John Holland, who also figures in the plot of 2 *Seven Deadly Sins*, and also—though it has hitherto passed unnoticed[1]—in the stage-direction which heads 4. 2. in 2 *Henry VI*. The said direction, which runs 'Enter Beuis, and Iohn Holland,' refers to two prentice supporters of Jack Cade, whose names never occur in the text, so that it is possible that 'Beuis' who gets a second entry at 4. 7. 21, this time under the title of 'George,' may be yet another actor's name.

Turning to *The Shrew* itself we come upon quite a crop of little clues in addition to the 'Sincklo' just referred to. We may begin with a passage from 4. 2. 67–72 which runs as follows in the Folio:

> *Tra.* If he be credulous, and truſt my tale,
> Ile make him glad to ſeeme *Vincentio*,
> And giue aſſurance to *Baptiſta Minola*.
> As if he were the right *Vincentio*.
> *Par.* Take me[2] your loue, and then let me alone.
>
> *Enter a Pedant.*
>
> *Ped.* God ſaue you ſir.

It seems clear that 'Par.' stands for a player's name which was written in the margin of the prompt-book opposite to the stage-direction to indicate the actor of the Pedant's part[3], and was then mistaken for a prefix to the previous line. The 'Par' may of course be a contraction; but if so the only recorded actor's name of the period for which it might stand is that of Thomas Parsons, who as a boy acting for the Admiral's men in

[1] Dr Greg informs me that Sir Edmund Chambers has recently drawn attention to it in an unprinted paper read before the Oxford Bibliographical Society.

[2] A misprint for 'in' (inne).

[3] I owe this explanation to Dr Greg.

1598 is surely out of the question. If on the other hand it be a name in full, William Parr, who first appears in the plot of 1 *Tamar Cam*, performed in 1602 by the Admiral's men (though the 1598 entry 'A cloth of silver for Parr,' in Henslowe's *Diary* looks like an earlier reference to him), and who turns up again in 1618 as a joint-lessee of the Fortune Theatre, would seem to fit the case well enough. More interesting is the name 'Nicke' which appears as a speech-heading for the messenger at 3. 1. 82. Following Steevens most commentators have identified him with Nicholas Tooley, who figures in the list of the 'Principal Actors' at the beginning of the First Folio. As Nick is a common name the identification is hazardous, though possible. It is also possible that the boy 'Nick' who is cast for two female parts in the plot of 2 *Seven Deadly Sins* was the same actor. In any event, it can hardly be doubted that the 'Nicke' of *The Shrew* reappears in the text of the *Contention* (1594) where he takes the part that John Holland took in 2 *Henry VI*. He too is accompanied by a 'George,' though it is interesting to note that he is far more conspicuous in the Jack Cade scenes than was John Holland; the text of the *Contention* having been obviously adapted to give him more 'fat.' Nor, we think, was Nick's part in *The Shrew* confined to that of the messenger in 3. 1. 'Nicholas' for instance is named in the list of Petruchio's servants in 4. 1., and his two words of greeting to Grumio (4. 1. 100) are headed 'Nick' in the Folio. Furthermore, as we shall note presently, he probably also played Biondello. Now if we could be certain that this 'Nick' was indeed Nicholas Tooley, and that his name in the 1623 text goes back to 1592–4, his presence with the Pembroke men would be a fact of considerable significance, since it would render it possible that Burbage was a member of the company also. Nicholas Tooley, who became a full 'sharer' in the King's company about 1605[1]—for though he does not appear among the nine principals mentioned in the royal letters patent of 1603, he is named by Augustine Phillips as his 'fellow' in a will made in 1605—refers to Burbage in his own will as his former 'master,' which implies that he had once been Burbage's apprentice. Apprenticeship was a regular channel in Elizabethan times to the acting profession, and almost every actor of importance would have one or more 'boys' attached to him in this way, and these boys if they did well would in course of time grow up to become sharers of the company and have their own apprentices. There is no difficulty in supposing that Tooley who became a sharer in 1605 had been a boy-player a dozen years earlier. And if Burbage's boy was acting with the Pembroke men, Burbage himself may also have been of the troupe. We have seen that Burbage was not with Alleyn's touring company of Strange's men; he cannot have been playing in London at his father's 'Theatre' because of the plague; it seems natural enough therefore to look for him among the Pembroke men.

A similar line of argument, on the principle of 'follow man find master,' would lead us to include in the cast one William Bird, *alias* Borne, a not unimportant though obscure player, who like Jeffes and Spencer came to the Admiral's men in 1597 from the second Pembroke's company after they broke up, and was in 1601–2 engaged with Samuel Rowley in revising plays for Henslowe, among them Marlowe's *Doctor Faustus*[2]. His name nowhere appears in the text of *The Shrew*,

[1] Chambers (ii. 346–7) thinks 'he probably joined the company in 1605,' but gives no reason for his opinion. Considering his early connexion with Burbage, Tooley is far more likely to have been a member of the company for many years.

[2] *Henslowe's Diary*, ed. Greg, ii. 241–2.

which, however, heads the single line that Katharina's haberdasher has to speak (4. 3. 63) with the prefix 'Fel.' instead of the 'Hab.' we should expect; and if this 'Fel.' be taken, not as a contraction of 'fellow,' but, on the analogy of 'Par.' at 4. 2. 72, as a proper name, the only one that suggests itself is that of William Felle, who though not known as a player appears in Henslowe's *Diary* under the year 1599 as William Bird's 'man.' And once again supposing the man to be taking a small part or two with the Pembroke men in 1592–3, his master may well have been with him, acting in a more important rôle. The identification is a hazardous one, but could it be established important consequences would follow, inasmuch as Rowley's collaborator in 1601 might easily be his collaborator in 1593, and the presence of Bird and Rowley together with the degenerate company that followed the bankruptcy of the Pembroke men in the summer of that year would amply account for the 'reported' texts above spoken of.

Other possible actors' names besides Nicholas are to be found in the list of Petruchio's servants. Gabriel, of course, suggests Gabriel Spencer. Curtis, moreover, the leader of the group, possesses a strangely English-sounding name for a steward of a country house near Verona, bandying jests with a Grumio. When, however, we discover that one Curtis was a minor actor in the King's company, who took small parts in *The Two Noble Kinsmen* (1613)[1], the origin of the character in *The Shrew* finds at least a possible explanation. Similarly 'Peter,' who after Curtis is the servant with most to say in this scene, is almost certainly an actor's name, since he reappears in the Folio text at 4. 4. 68 as a 'mute' servant, this time not of Petruchio's but of Tranio's, and Sir Edmund Chambers actually goes so far as to

[1] *T.N.K.* 4. 2. 75 'Enter Messenger, Curtis'; 5. 3. 1, Curtis named as an attendant.

include him in his List of Actors, though he can throw no further light upon him[1]. And if Nicholas, Curtis and Peter be real names, conceivably some of the other players who acted as servants of Petruchio's household may have used their own names on the stage. However that may be, one thing is certain about the cast that played *The Shrew* according to the F. version, viz. that it was rich in boy actors. Besides those required for the three female parts, who all appear on the stage together in the last scene and therefore could not be doubled, Biondello was played by a boy, as is clear from the dialogue at 4. 4. 8–9[2], and what is even more remarkable Grumio must have been a boy likewise, if the jests upon his stature at 4. 1. 1–30 possess any point at all, while Petruchio's abuse of the Tailor seems likewise to indicate a boy actor (v. note 4. 3. 109–110). We are inclined to think that the part of Biondello was taken by 'Nick,' since Biondello might easily have been doubled with the small parts we have already attached to 'Nick's' name, while the prominence of the same actor in the *Contention* and the possibility that he was Tooley render him a likely candidate for the important rôle of Tranio's servant. But we can feel more certain of the identity of Grumio's impersonator, seeing that in *A Shrew*, the Pembroke text in its debased later form, the actor's name 'Sander' (or 'San') appears first as the principal Player in the Induction and later both in dialogue and speech-headings as the actual name of the character who corresponds with Grumio in the original. Now 'Sander,' who (like 'Nick') figures in the plot of 2 *Seven Deadly Sins* and in the *Contention*, almost certainly stands for Alexander Cooke, who (like Tooley) had

[1] In Aug. 1593 Alleyn sends a letter and a horse to his father-in-law Henslowe by a servant named Peter. *Henslowe's Diary*, ii. 302.

[2] See also the S.D. at 2. 1. 38.

grown up to be a sharer in the King's company by 1605 (cf. pp. 181–82). Like Tooley, yet again, Cooke had once been an apprentice boy-actor, and must have been such in 1593 if the identification with 'Sander' be admitted. In this case, however, his possible presence with Pembroke's men would not imply the presence of his master also, inasmuch as his master was Heminge who, as we have seen, was playing at the time with Alleyn. Nevertheless, this is no exception to the principle of 'follow man find master,' for *ex hypothesi* Alleyn's troupe and the Pembroke men were not two separate companies (though each probably agreed to take its own financial risks), but two branches of the same company, or rather of the same amalgamation. There would, therefore, be nothing surprising at finding Heminge in one section and a prentice of his in the other. It is the fact that Burbage is not known to have been playing with Alleyn that would render likely his presence with the Pembroke men, if that troupe included 'Nick' Tooley.

B. *The original manuscript*

The foregoing section is a digression from our main argument, to which we must now return. If that argument be sound, then the transmitted text of *The Shrew* was printed from a transcript made for the Pembroke men in 1592 and not from what the publishers of the Folio call the 'first original,' which *ex hypothesi* must have been left behind in London in the hands of Shakespeare or some other representative of the Strange-Chamberlain men, when Pembroke's men first went on tour. What happened to this 'first original'? Why was it not used as copy by the Folio compositors? Did it differ in any important respects from the transcript which Heminge and Condell saw fit to hand over to Jaggard in 1623? These are important questions, upon which it is impossible at this time of day to say anything definite, but which nevertheless are worth posing if only by way of exploring possibilities.

The three questions all hang together. For if, in the first place, there was no important difference, in the eyes of Heminge and Condell, between the 1592 transcript and the original—supposing they both reposed in the Globe library in 1623—the players would naturally hand over the transcript to Jaggard, just as they preferred (in the case of other plays) to deliver him a printed quarto collated with the playhouse manuscript to surrendering the manuscript itself. Differences, moreover, which seem to us important, even vital, would not necessarily appear so to them. Indeed, it does not by any means follow that they would hand over the most Shakespearian of two texts, provided they considered them both good acting copy. For instance, we have seen reason for thinking that the copy for *The Merchant of Venice* given to the printers in 1600 was only a transcript, and not even a faithful transcript, of Shakespeare's original; yet it was a prompt-book, and was actually so entered in the Stationers' Register, as Dr W. W. Greg has recently pointed out[1], while the employment of the resultant quarto as the copy for the Folio text would suggest that in the eyes of the players it was at least as good a prompt-book as the other[2]. Supposing then in 1623 two volumes were found in the theatre library, each engrossed *The booke of the Taming of the Shrew*, the chances are that the one traditionally used for Globe performances would get into print, even though it was a transcript and the other was a Shakespearian holograph. It is not necessary, therefore, to our argument to dispose of the first original

[1] *The Library*, March 1927, pp. 384–5.

[2] In the case of *Hamlet* Heminge and Condell clearly considered the playhouse transcript better copy than the fuller, though less actable, Shakespearian text which had got into print in 1605.

by imagining that it was lost, as that of *The Winter's Tale* seems to have been lost[1], or burnt in the celebrated fire which consumed the Globe playhouse in 1613, though of course it may have disappeared in either of these two ways.

In the case of *The Merchant* the internal evidence which pointed to transcription also led us to believe that the text had been tampered with, certainly in one place and probably in others, by a hand not Shakespeare's. A reference to the notes below, especially 4. 1. 170 S.D., and 4. 4. 17 S.D., will show that something of the same kind may have happened to *The Shrew*, inasmuch as there appears to have been adaptation of the text after the transcript had been made for the Pembroke men. Moreover in the garbled *A Shrew* we have a piece of external evidence which suggests a further and still more important difference between the Folio version and Shakespeare's original. I have already recorded my agreement with Mr Alexander's contention that *A Shrew* was based upon a memorised reconstruction of Shakespeare's play. His position is even stronger than would appear from the article in which he sets it forth, inasmuch as it is founded upon evidence printed in *Notes and Queries*[2] by one Samuel Hickson over three-quarters of a century ago, evidence to which Mr Alexander of course refers but which limitations of space forbad him to repeat at length. Hickson cites no less than seven passages from *A Shrew* which when set alongside of parallel passages from *The Shrew* are clearly seen to have been reported from the latter text by some person or persons who have missed the point of what they were trying to remember; and the interesting thing about these passages is that they all come from the Petruchio-Katharina scenes of *The Shrew*, in other words from those portions of

[1] Pollard, *Shakespeare Folios and Quartos*, p. 135.

[2] *Notes and Queries*, vol. i. pp. 345–7, March 30, 1850.

the play which even the most radical criticism ascribes unhesitatingly to Shakespeare's pen[1]. *A Shrew*, therefore, gives us what the players could remember of Shakespeare's play, worked up into an acting text by a dramatist, or dramatists, very much under the influence of Marlowe. Was the play they had in mind identical with that which has been transmitted to us by the Folio, or was it different? Taken as a whole *A Shrew* is so remote from the play as we know it, that it affords a very insecure foothold for speculation. It would be absurd, for example, to argue that the absence from the 1594 text of certain familiar scenes or episodes indicates their absence also from the version behind the reconstruction, since such absence is most easily explained by forgetfulness. There is, however, one striking divergence in structure between the two texts which is at least worthy of consideration.

Everyone who has studied *The Shrew* has remarked upon the strange way in which the business of Christopher Sly, which begins so bravely, drops out of notice altogether after the end of the first scene of the play. As Fleay remarks, 'This Induction is most clumsily managed: there is no provision for getting Sly off the stage. Shakespeare could never have been guilty of this blunder[2].' In *A Shrew*, on the other hand, the Sly plot is carried right through to the end. At the conclusion of the scene that corresponds with 5. 1. in the better text Sly drops asleep once more, and the Lord bids his servants bear him back to the place where they found him, while the drama is rounded off with an awakening, which reminds one strongly of Bottom's, and the departure of Sly to tame the shrew at his own hearth-stone. It seems to us extremely improbable that

[1] Hickson's seven parallels are quoted in the notes: 2. 1. 172–3; 4. 3. 69–72, 123–6, 133–5, 167–72; 5. 2. 176–9, 184–5.

[2] *Shakespeare Manual*, p. 175.

the 'remnant' company can have invented these extra Sly scenes. On the contrary, seeing that such scenes render two players (Sly and the Lord) incapable of taking any part in the main play, a provincial company would appear to have every inducement to cut them out. In other words, we think it at least possible that the reconstruction was in this regard faithful to the original, that Shakespeare himself intended Sly to sit the play out and revert to beggary at the end, and that in the interest of theatrical convenience these intentions have been frustrated in the text that has come down to us. And while the excision of these original Sly scenes may have been carried out for the Pembroke men in 1592, it must be remembered that a few strokes of the pen would suffice to rid the transcript of them at any time, and for any performance, between that date and 1623.

On another question, that of a possible revision by Shakespeare of an earlier play or of his collaboration with one or more other dramatists, something has been said in the Introduction (pp. x–xii)[1]. For the theory of collaboration, as we have there seen, there is little to be urged, and though there are the usual marks of revision, such as fossil verse (e.g. notes 1. 2. 39–42, 5. 1. 72) and dramatic loose-ends (e.g. head-note 5. 1.), these may have been due to the post-Shakespearian adapter for whose presence there is some evidence, as we have just pointed out. On the other hand, the character and dramatic fortunes of Hortensio present certain remarkable features which seem difficult to account for except on the theory that in a pre-Shakespearian form of the play his rôle was more conspicuous than in the received text, and, indeed, comprised a good many of the speeches which

[1] For a recent attempt to work out this side of the subject, in reply to Professor E. P. Kuhl referred to in our Introduction (p. xi), v. *The Revision of the Folio Text of 'The Taming of the Shrew,'* by Florence H. Ashton (*Phil. Quarterly*, vol. vi. no. 2).

are now assigned to Tranio. In the first act, both as the rival of Gremio and the friend of Petruchio he takes the centre of the stage. But no sooner does he disguise himself as Licio than he seems oddly enough officially to drop out of the running as suitor. For example, he takes no part in the bidding for Bianca's hand at the end of 2. 1. As he had appeared as Licio earlier in the scene—he goes out at l. 168—, and reappears, also disguised at the opening of the scene that follows (3. 1.), it would no doubt be theatrically awkward to bring him in clad as Hortensio to bid against Gremio and Tranio at 2. 1. 324. This, however, will not account for the fact that in the first half of 3. 2. Tranio has completely stepped into his shoes, speaks of Petruchio as if he were his life-long friend, and treats him as such when he appears; in short, behaves exactly as if he were Hortensio. Almost equally strange is Hortensio's visit to Petruchio's house in 4. 3., after assuring Tranio in the previous scene that he would 'be married to a wealthy widow ere three days pass.' It is true that Tranio prepares us for this visit by a jest to Lucentio and Bianca about Hortensio going to 'the training-school'; but his knowledge of Hortensio's intentions must have been arrived at by divination, since Hortensio himself tells him nothing except that he is about to marry. Lastly Petruchio himself in 4. 5. is able to inform Vincentio all about his son's betrothal to Bianca, although he cannot possibly as far as the text enlightens us have known anything about it[1]. In other words, we suspect that Shakespeare was as usual revising an old play, that his chief interest lay in the Petruchio-Katharina scenes, that in expanding these he was obliged to cut down the plot elsewhere, and that the deleted material would have told us more

[1] v. note 4. 5. 63. For much in this paragraph we are indebted to P. A. Daniel's *Time-Analysis of Shakespeare's Plays*, pp 162–9.

about Hortensio and perhaps also about Gremio. We suspect too that he left a good many of the scenes as he found them, and that some of the prose clown-dialogue which he found was from the hand of Thomas Nashe (cf. notes 1. 2. 78; 3. 2. 43–61).

However this may be, one fact of primary importance emerges from what has been said above. Whether Shakespeare created *The Shrew* or recreated it, the work he did upon it must have been finished before the Pembroke men went on tour in the summer of 1592, or at any rate before 2 May 1594 when *A Shrew*, which is demonstrably based upon the Shakespearian play, was first entered in the Stationers' Register. If the reader be prepared to accept this conclusion, let him not shut his eyes to the consequences. One of them is that Shakespeare at this early date was already capable of the verse we find, for instance, in Petruchio's speech at the end of 4. 1. or Katharina's at the end of 5. 2. Surely not a remarkable feat for the greatest of all poets at the age of 27 to 30, and yet one that orthodox Shakespearian criticism will, unless we are mistaken, find it very difficult to credit.

[1928] D. W.

NOTES

All significant departures from the Folio text, including emendations in punctuation, are recorded; the name of the critic who first suggested an accepted reading being placed in brackets. Illustrative spellings and misprints are quoted from the Good Quarto texts, or from the Folio where no Good Quarto exists. The line-numeration for reference to plays not yet issued in this edition is that used in Bartlett's *Concordance*.

F., unless otherwise specified, stands for the First Folio; T.I. for the Textual Introduction to be found in the *Tempest* volume; Bond for *The Taming of the Shrew* ed. by Prof. Warwick Bond (Arden Shakespeare), 1904; Sh. Hand for *Shakespeare's Hand in the play of 'Sir Thomas More'* (Camb. Univ. Press, 1923); Ham. Sp. and Misp. for *Spellings and Misprints in the Second Quarto of Hamlet* (Essays and Studies by members of the English Association, vol. x); N.E.D. for *The New English Dictionary*; Sh. Eng. for *Shakespeare's England*; S.D. for stage-direction; G. for Glossary.

Characters in the Play. A list was first supplied by Rowe. For *Christopher Sly* v. head-note Ind. i.; for *Curtis* v. p. 118; for *Nicholas* and *Peter* v. pp. 116–18.

Acts and Scenes. The F. divisions are eccentric and may be given in full. The text is headed, like others in the F., 'Actus primus. Scœna Prima,' but no provision is made for the Induction, a heading which was first introduced by Pope. There is no trace of 'Actus secundus,' the next F. division being 'Actus Tertia' (*sic*), which coincides with the modern 'act 3.' The headings 'Actus Quartus. Scena Prima' (at 4. 3.) and 'Actus Quintus' (at 5. 2.) complete the tale.

Punctuation. Very mediocre in this text. The specimens quoted from the F. in the notes that follow prove that most if not all the stops were supplied by someone who often possessed only dim ideas of the sense of the original. The frequency of the grammatical, as distinct from the dramatic, use of the full stop suggests the printing-house. On the other hand, the unusually large number of transpositions of the pointing at the end of two consecutive lines suggests that the compositor had stops in his copy to transpose.

Stage-directions. All original S.D.s are quoted in the notes. For their textual interest, which is considerable, v. pp. 99–104.

Induction i.

S.D. F. 'Enter Begger and Hostes, Christophero Sly.' All Sly's speeches are headed 'Beg.' in F., and it looks as if 'Christophero Sly' were an explanatory marginal note by the prompter. The Italian name for this very English beggar is curious; it recurs at Ind. ii. 5, 73, though at l. 18 of the same scene he calls himself 'Christopher.' *Before an alehouse* etc. (Theobald).

1. *feeze* F. 'pheeze' We follow, as usual, the spelling of N.E.D.

5. *paucas pallabris* v. G. The expression formed part of the patter of the common juggler, and no doubt other rogues, of the period; cf. Sh.Eng. i. 541. But Sly may have got it from *The Spanish Tragedy*, 3. 14. 118 (cf. note l. 8 below).

let the world slide A summary of the beggar's philosophy; Sly repeats it at Ind. ii. 142.

8. *Go by, S. Jeronimy* A misquotation from Kyd's *Spanish Tragedy*, the hero of which at one point (3. 12. 31) mutters to himself 'Hieronimo beware; go by, go by.' This passage, as Kyd's editor Dr Boas remarks, was in Shakespeare's day 'quoted over and over again, as the stock phrase to imply impatience of anything disagreeable, inconvenient or old-fashioned' (Boas, *Kyd's Works*, p. 406). That Sly should confuse

Kyd's Hieronimo with S. Jerome (Hieronymus) or Jeremy the prophet, is merely in keeping with the learning that harks back to Richard Conqueror. Sly, like Kyd's hero, is of course addressing himself; he sees danger in the Hostess' eye and bids himself beware.

8-9. *go to thy cold bed, and warm thee* Another echo from *The Spanish Tragedy*, act 2, sc. 5 which deals with the discovery by old Hieronimo of his murdered son and begins 'What out-cries pluck me from my naked bed?' Cf. *Lear*, 3. 4. 48. That Sly finds a veritable 'cold bed' at this point is evident from ll. 31–2 below.

10. *thirdborough* (Theobald) F. 'Headborough' Sly's retort makes Theobald's emendation certain, and since *th* and *h* were liable to confusion the F. error is explicable graphically.

13. *boy* an insult, not a mere piece of drunken oblivion; v. G.

14. *and kindly* i.e. by all means; v. G. 'kindly.'

S.D. F. 'Falles aſleepe./Winde hornes. Enter a Lord from hunting, with his traine.'

15–29. This little hunting episode bears a close resemblance to *M.N.D.* 4. 1. 102–26, which describes the hunting expedition of Duke Theseus.

16. *Broach* F. 'Brach' The F. reading is impossible, because (i) it leaves the sentence without a verb, and (ii) it involves an ugly repetition with 'brach' in l. 17. Many emendations have been offered, e.g. 'leech,' 'bathe,' 'trash,' 'brace,' none of which except the last take any account of the *ductus litterarum*. The reading we propose, 'Broach' (sp. 'broch'), involves the least possible alteration, and fits the context well, since to broach means to bleed and blood-letting would seem a good remedy for an 'embossed' (i.e. dead-beat) hound to the veterinary science of the age.

19. *at the hedge corner* This 'seems to indicate,' writes Mr Fortescue, 'that the Lord had been coursing the hare' (Sh.Eng. ii. 349).

the coldest fault A 'fault' is a break in the scent, and strictly speaking it is the scent which is 'cold' (cf. *Tw. Nt.* 2. 5. 134 'he is now at a cold scent'), but 'cold fault' is a common hunting expression of the time. Shakespeare describes in *V. A.* 691–94 how the hare runs among sheep or conies to put the hounds off the scent:

> For there his smell with others being mingled,
> The hot scent-snuffing hounds are driven to doubt,
> Ceasing their clamorous cry till they have singled
> With much ado the cold fault cleanly out.

22. *the merest loss* v. G. 'mere.'

31–2. *He breathes...soundly* F. prints as prose. *my lord.* So F.

34. *Grim death...image* The filthy beggar lies like one dead.

37. *clothes,* F. 'cloathes:' *fingers,* F. 'fingers:'

48. *burn sweet wood* etc. Cf. *Ado,* 1. 3. 55–6 'as I was smoking a musty room.'

52. *And with...reverence* F. places this line within brackets.

56. *ewer,* F. 'Ewer:'

61. *disease:* F. 'diſeaſe,

62. *lunatic;* F. 'Lunaticke,

63. *he is, say.* In the 1928 edition I accepted the emendation 'he is Sly, say' proposed by Dr Johnson, who noted 'the likeness in writing "Sly" and "say" produced the omission.' But Mr A. T. S. Sampson pointed out in a private letter (1. xii. 48) that the lord had not so far heard Sly's name, and that 'is', taken with the preceding line, makes clear sense:

> Persuade him that he *hath been* lunatic;
> And when he says he *is* [i.e. lunatic], say that he dreams.

65. *do it kindly* i.e. do it naturally.

67. *husbanded with modesty* managed without excess; cf. *Ham.* 3. 2. 21 'o'erstep not the modesty of nature.'

68. *warrant* Here, as often elsewhere in Shakespeare, a monosyllable; cf. *A.Y.L.* 4. 1. 73 (note).

72. S.D. F. 'Sound trumpets.' Cf. *Ham.* (Q 2) 2. 2. 385 'A florish,' and *M.N.D.* (F.) 5. 1. 107 'Flor. Trum.'—before the entry of players.

73. F. gives no 'exit' for the serving-man

75. S.D. F. 'Enter Seruingman.'

78. S.D. F. 'Enter Players.'—after l. 77. It is unnecessary to point out how appropriate this episode would be in a play taken on tour by a travelling company which would hope to 'offer service' to many a lord.

81. *So please* etc. F. heads this '2. Player,' though no '1. Player' is named.

87. *I think 'twas Soto* etc. This is an important, if puzzling, passage as regards stage-history. F. heads the speech 'Sincklo,' thereby informing us that it was spoken by John Sincler or Sincklo, a minor actor of Shakespeare's company, who if the evidence we have about him were taken at its face value would have been on the stage for over 30 years. This evidence consists of the chance occurrence of his name in prompt-books and in one of the extant theatrical plots. The last-mentioned, the plot of 2 *Seven Deadly Sins*, which was probably being played by Strange's men 1590–2, contains the earliest reference to him, and shows him acting in turn as a keeper, a soldier, a captain and a warder. In Shakespearian texts his name occurs on three occasions: 3 *Hen. VI* (F.) 3. 1. 1, where he plays a forester; 2 *Hen. IV* (Q. 1600) 5. 4. 1, where he acts the Beadle with Doll in custody; and the instance before us, which likewise assigns him a small speaking part. The editors of the *Cambridge Shakespeare* (1863), for some reason not given, believed that he probably took the part of Lucentio in the present play. Outside Shakespeare, his name occurs as acting in the Induction to Marston's *Malecontent* (1604), while the reference to Soto before us points at first blush to a play of Fletcher's which is

dated as late as 1620; Soto 'a farmer's eldest son' being a character in *Women Pleased*.

The passage, therefore, leaves us with two alternatives: either (i) that ll. 82–87 are an insertion (they could, in fact, be omitted without any injury to the text) made after Shakespeare's death at some revival of *The Shrew* shortly before the publication of F.; or (ii) that *Women Pleased* was itself based upon an earlier text belonging to Shakespeare's company and that Sincklo was playing Soto in this earlier version sometime about 1591–2. We incline to the second alternative for three reasons. In the first place Fletcher's play contains a character named Lopez, who in 1. 2. speaks lines reminiscent of Marlowe's *Jew of Malta*, and both these facts point to a date nearer to 1590 than 1620 (cf. *M.V.* pp. 116–18). In the second place, Soto is an important rôle, far more important than any other attached to Sincklo's name; if then he was playing this part about 1620, and was being given a gratuitous congratulation on his performance in another King's men play, surely it is strange that his name does not appear in the list of Principal Actors at the beginning of the Folio? And in the third place, the description of the Soto part which the Lord gives does not tally exactly with that in Fletcher's play, as Tyrwhitt noted long ago. The Soto in *Women Pleased* dresses himself in his master's clothes with the intention of wooing his master's lady, who is confined in a high tower, but is shot (or imagines he is shot) by another lover when about to make the attempt. Thus he never 'wooed the gentlewoman' at all, and thus the Lord who remembers the wooing-scene particularly is apparently singularly wide of the mark. Yet had Soto, who is a country clown, actually wooed the lady, it might well have been a memorable scene for the laughter it caused. In short, we suggest that the Lord in *The Shrew* is referring to the original play and to a scene which

Fletcher dispensed with on revision. That Soto was a well-known character long before 1620, appears from a reference to him in the Oxford 'Twelfe-Night Merriment' *Narcissus* (c. 1602), to which Dr Greg draws my attention. The passage (ll. 510–11) runs:

least you should counte me for a Sot-o
(A very pretty figure called pars pro toto).

96. *merry passion* outbreak of mirth.

101. *take them to the buttery* etc. Cf. *Ham.* 2. 2. 546–59. The suggestion that players deserved generous treatment at the hands of patrons is naturally not infrequent in Elizabethan drama. 'My Lord Cardinal's players' in *Sir Thomas More* are provided with a drink before playing and a 'reward' and supper afterwards.

103. S.D. F. 'Exit one with the Players.'

104. *Barthol'mew my page* etc. In an age when boys always played women on the stage, there would seem nothing remarkable in this passage.

111. *accomplishèd:* F. 'accompliſhed,' 112. *do,* F. 'do:'—transposed pointing.

129. S.D. F. 'Exit a ſeruingman.'

137. S.D. F. gives no 'exeunt.'

Induction ii.

S.D. F. 'Enter aloft the drunkard with attendants, ſome with apparel, Baſon and Ewer, & other appurtenances, & Lord.' Theobald read 'A bedchamber in the Lord's house.'

The F. S.D. makes it clear, as Malone first noted, that Sly and the rest were intended to appear in the gallery above and at the back of the stage. It is also clear, as Sir E. Chambers observes, that the actors 'move about a chamber and occupy a considerable space' (*Eliz. Stage*, iii. 94). We must suppose, therefore, that Sly, etc. are 'discovered' in a set scene on the upper stage by the drawing aside of curtains. This suggested arrangement has the merit of helping to explain the disappearance of the 'presenters' before the end of the play. At some point of the action the curtain is closed—that is all. Cf. note 1. 1. 252 S.D.

asleep in a chair We take this from *A Shrew*; it is clear from ll. 37–9 below that Sly is not discovered in bed.

2. *lordship* (F 2) F. 'Lord'

9. *backs,* F. 'backes:' *legs,* F. 'legges:'

18. *Sly's son* (F 2) F. 'Sies sonne'

Burton-heath Lee, following Malone, identifies this with Barton-on-the-Heath, about 16 miles from Stratford, and the home of Shakespeare's aunt, Edmund Lambert's wife, and her sons (Lee, *Life*, ed. 1916, p. 236). It seems clear that Shakespeare was drawing upon his own home memories in his portrait of Sly.

21. *Marian Hacket...of Wincot* Cf. ll. 89–90 below 'Cicely Hacket...the woman's maid of the house.' Lee (*Life*, p. 237) writes: 'Wincot was the familiar designation of three small Warwickshire villages, and a good claim has been set up on behalf of each to be the scene of Sly's exploits.' The first is one about four miles from Stratford, forming part of the parish of Quinton, the registers of which record the baptism of a daughter to Robert Hacket on Nov. 21, 1591. The second is Wilmecote (pron. Wincot), at some distance from Stratford, near Tamworth, yet definitely identified with Shakespeare's Wincot in 1658 by the Warwickshire poet, Sir Aston Cockain, in verses addressed to 'Mr Clement Fisher of Wincott,' which begin

> Shakespeare your Wincot ale hath much renowned
> That fox'd a Beggar so (by chance was found
> Sleeping) that there needed not many a word
> To make him to believe he was a Lord.

The third is Wilmcote, the native place of Shakespeare's mother.

22. *xiiii. d.* The F. reading seems preferable to the prim 'fourteen pence' of modern texts.

23–4. *the lyingest knave in Christendom* As Fleay notes, the expression recurs in 2 *Hen. VI*, 2. 1. 126.

25. *here's—* For the suggestion of 'enter a pot of small ale' to explain this exclamation we are indebted to Bond (note Ind. ii. 1). Sly cannot be actually 'bestraught' while there is ale in the world. Cf. note, l. 75 below.

26. The servants' speeches, hitherto headed '1, 2, 3 Ser.', are from this point headed '1, 2, 3 Man.' Does not the style change at the same place? The fifty lines or so that follow seem extraordinarily Marlowesque, while it is to be noted that Sly himself takes to blank verse.

29. *lunacy.* So F. 34. *beck.* So F.

35. S.D. F. 'Muſick.'

36. *sing.* So F. 39. *Semiramis.* So F.

40. *ground:* F. 'ground.'

42. *pearl.* So F. 44. *lark.* So F.

73. *Christophero* (F 2) F. 'Chriſtopher'

75. *once again a pot* etc. This 'again' lends strong support to Bond's conjecture at l. 25. *o'th' smallest ale* The superlative gives us the drunkard's accustomed supplicating tone to the exasperated hostess.

76. S.D. Capell reads 'presenting the Ewer, etc.'

82. *of all that time* i.e. for all that time; cf. *L.L.L.* 1. 1. 43 'of all the day.'

87–8. *present her at the leet...quarts* v. G. 'leet.' Malone notes that the following, among other articles of matters 'enquirable and presentable and also punishable in a leet,' occurs in Kitchen on *Courts* (ed. 1663): 'Also if tipplers sell by cups and dishes or measures sealed, or not sealed, is inquirable'; quoting at the same time from *Characterisimi or Lenton's Leasures*, 1623: 'He an informer transforms himselfe into several shapes, to avoid suspicion of inne-holders, and inwardly joyes at the sight of a blacke pot or iugge, knowing that their sale by sealed quarts, spoyles his market.' In a word, Sly threatens to turn informer.

93–4. *Stephen Sly...Pimpernell* 'There was a genuine Stephen Sly, who was in the dramatist's day a self-assertive citizen of Stratford; and "Greece," whence "old John Naps" derived his cognomen, is an obvious misreading of Greet, a hamlet by Winchcourt, in Gloucestershire, not far removed from Shakespeare's native town' (Lee, *Life*, p. 238).

99. S.D. F. 'Enter Lady with Attendants.'—after l. 98.

116. S.D. Neither F. nor any mod. ed. gives an 'exeunt' for the servants here, though one is required not only in response to Sly's command but also in order to clear the gallery of all but the three 'presenters': Sly, the disguised page, and 1 Servant. Cf. note 1. 1. 246, S.D.

120. *set:* F. 'ſet.'

127. S.D. F. 'Enter a Meſſenger.' As '1 Servant' is still 'on' at the end of 1. 1. we give him a re-entry here.

131–32. *Seeing too much sadness...frenzy* Cf. *M.N.D.* 3. 2. 97 (note). Bond cites *King John*, 3. 3. 42–44:

> Or if that surly spirit, melancholy,
> Had baked thy blood and made it heavy-thick,
> Which else runs tickling up and down the veins.

136. *play it. Is not* (Capell) F. 'play, it is not'

136–37. *commodity* F. 'Comontie' The F. reading gives us a meaningless blunder, whereas 'commodity' explains 'household stuff' (l. 139) and makes clear the movement of Sly's mind. He knows two kinds of 'commodity': stage-tricks and furniture. Further, our reading receives support from *A Shrew*, the following passage of which shows that the 'commodity' jest had taken firm hold of the actors' memories though it has got displaced (sc. i. 57–62):

Enter two of the players with packs at their backs, and a boy.

Lord. Now sirs, what store of plaies haue you?
San. Marrie my lord you maie haue a Tragicall or a comoditie, or what you will.
The other. A Comedie thou shouldst say, souns thout shame vs all.

142. S.D. F. 'Flouriſh.'—at the head of 1. 1.

1. 1.

S.D. F. 'Flouriſh. Enter Lucentio, and his man Triano.' For the sp. 'Triano' v. p. 101. Our setting of this, the principal scene, corresponds closely with that for the Mart of Ephesus in *Errors*, and the two scenes have obviously been conceived by the dramatist in the same fashion. In stage-terms, there are two doors, one standing for the entry into the square, the other for Hortensio's house (1. 2.) or Lucentio's house (4. 2. etc.), together with a third entry under the gallery, which stands for Baptista's house. The arrangement works well, except in 3. 2., where its breakdown is due to scene-splicing (v. note 3. 2. 125 S.D.) and is confirmed by 5. 1. 9–10.

2. *Padua, nursery of arts* The university of Padua was founded in 1228. It is clear from ll. 3, 42, 229 and 1. 2. 47–9 that Padua is imagined as a sea-port. Cf. the geography of *Two Gent.* (e.g. notes 1. 1. 54, 2. 3. 34–5). In similar fashion Kyd in the *Spanish Tragedy* (3. 14. 11) writes as if Lisbon and Madrid were connected by sea.

12. *world,* F. 'world:' 13. *Bentivolii;* F. 'Bentiuolij,'—transposed pointing.

13. *Vincentio* (Hanmer) F. 'Vincentio's'—caught from the next line.

14. *brought* (F 2) F. 'brough'

17–8. *study/Virtue*, F. 'ſtudie,/Vertue' The shifting of the comma adds greatly to the force of the passage. We owe this suggestion to Mr Sydney Preston.

18–20. *that part of philosophy...achieved* This is a clear reference to Aristotle's *Ethics*, and as Bond notes 'affords support to Blackstone's conjecture' at l. 32 (v. note).

24. *satiety* F. 'ſacietie'—an interesting spelling, revealing the contemporary pronunciation.

25. *Mi perdonato* (Clark and Wright). F. 'Me Pardonato' It is noteworthy that the Italian phrases in this play are confined to act 1 except for 'mercatantè' (4. 2. 63). 28. *philosophy*. So F.

32. *checks* i.e. restraints, counsels of moderation. Blackstone ingeniously conjectured 'ethics', which is both contextually attractive (v. note ll. 18–20 above), and graphically very possible, if we assume a sp. like 'ethecks.'

33. *Ovid* F. 'Ouid;'—which makes Ovid a devotee of Aristotle!

47. S.D. F. 'Enter Baptiſta with his two daughters, Katerina & Bianca, Gremio a Pantelowne, Hortentio ſiſter to Bianca. Lucen. Tranio, ſtand by.' An interesting S.D. (i) The misprint 'sister' for 'suter' (= suitor), which is corrected in F 2, is almost proof that the direction was written in Italian script, since the mistake would be very difficult to account for in the English hand. (ii) Note the elaborately descriptive character of the S.D. (v. pp. 99–100).

55. *To cart her* etc. Most edd. print this line as an aside, but Katharine's use of 'stale' shows that she overhears; for 'stales' (harlots) were commonly 'carted.'

rather: she's F. 'rather. She's'

58. *a stale of me among these mates* i.e. a laughing-stock of me among these rude fellows. For another meaning of 'stale' v. note l. 55 above. Possibly Katharine is also quibbling upon 'stale-mate.'

59. F. prints in two lines, dividing thus—'that?/No mates'

62. *Iwis* i.e. certainly. Most edd. print 'I wis' which is erroneous, and peculiarly unfortunate in a passage where the speaker is referring to herself in the third person.

it is not half way etc. The 'it' is marriage.

65. *paint your face* 'possibly with blood brought by scratching' (Bond).

68–71. Note the sudden occurrence of rhyming couplets.

78. *A pretty peat!* i.e. pretty, spoilt darling! Katharine's words are called forth by Baptista's tone and action.

79. *Put finger in the eye* Cf. *Errors*, 2. 2. 204 'To put the finger in the eye and weep.'

91. S.D. F. gives no 'exit.'

91–2. The broken line, followed by a line beginning 'And,' suggests a cut.

95. *youth.* So F.

101. S.D. F. 'Exit.'

103–4. F. divides thus: 'What...as though/(Belike)...to take,/And what...Ha.'

104. S.D. F. 'Exit.'

105–106. *your gifts...hold you* There is some quibble here, which we cannot explain.

107. *There! love* (Q. 1631 'There loue') F. 'Their loue' Collier first adopted the 1631 emendation, which Bond prefers, though he and most other mod. edd. follow F. The improvement in sense is great. Moreover, the exclamation 'There!' is characteristic of Gremio (cf. l. 56 above), while the 'their-there' confusion is one of the commonest in the Qq. Cf. *M.N.D.* 1. 1. 74 (note), *Ado*, 5. 1. 165 (note). The occurrence of 'ther' as a sp. both for 'there' and 'their' in the 'Shakespearian' Addition to *Sir Thomas More* indicates a possible source of the confusion (v. Sh.Hand, p. 138).

108. *blow our nails* i.e. wait patiently until new work comes along. Cf. *L.L.L.* 5. 2. 909 'And Dick the shepherd blows his nail,' and G. 'nail.'

109. *out:* F. 'out.'

our cake's dough proverbial expression of failure, cf. 5. 1. 135 and v. G. 'dough.'

116. *both—* F. 'both:'

131. *condition—* F. 'condition;'

137–38. *have to't* F. 'haue too t'

138. *Happy man be his dole!* v. G.

139. *the ring* A reference to 'riding (or 'running') at the ring,' with a quibble upon the wedding-ring.

141–42. *would I had given him the best horse* etc. Gremio carries on the idea of 'running at the ring.'

144. S.D. F. 'Exeunt ambo. Manet Tranio and Lucentio'

148. *likely;* F. 'likely.'

150. *love in idleness* 'Love-in-idleness' was another name for Heartsease, or the pansy, the flower, it will be remembered, which Puck and Oberon used to work their charms in *M.N.D.* The notion clearly was that when the heart was most at ease, most fancy-free, it was most vulnerable to the sudden shafts of Love.

153. *Anna to the Queen of Carthage* This rather forced introduction of a classical reference is unlike Shakespeare, but quite in the vein of Marlowe who with Nashe wrote the *Tragedie of Dido Queene of Carthage.* Lucentio confides in Tranio his sudden passion for Bianca as Dido confides in Anna her sudden passion for Aeneas (v. *Dido,* 3. 1.; McKerrow's *Nashe,* ii.).

was— F. 'was:'

159. *is not rated* is not to be scolded.

161. *Redime* etc. v. G. Tranio quotes from Lily's Latin syntax, and not from the original Terence (*Eunuchus,* 1. 1. 30), which runs 'Quid agas? nisi ut te redimas captum quam queas/Minimo.'

captum (F2) F. 'captam'

167. *the daughter of Agenor* Europa. The reference is to Ovid, *Met.* ii. 858.

178. *achieve her.* So F. 183. *he* (Dyce) F. 'ſhe'

188. *for my hand*=by my hand. 197. *full.* So F.

201. *stead,* F. 'ſted:' 202. *should:* F. 'ſhould,' —transposed pointing.

204. *mean man* (Capell) F. 'meaner man' This seems an improvement both in metre and sense. N.B. the writer of the S.D.s evidently read 'mean.' Cf. 2. 1. 38 S.D. (note). *Pisa.* So F.

206. *take my coloured hat* etc. In place of the servant's blue uniform; cf. 4. 1. 83 (note).

coloured (F 3) F. 'Conlord' Cf. *Cor.* (F.) 2. 3. 22 'Coulord' *cloak:* F. 'cloake,'

209–10. *So had you need* The broken line, with its no less broken sense, followed by a passage abruptly beginning 'In brief, sir,' suggests a cut. Why is it necessary to be so secretive with Biondello, or to invent a story to explain the change of dress? We are not told; and the thread is dropped, never to be taken up.

219. S.D. F. 'Enter Biondello.'

221–23. *Where...the news* F. prints this speech as prose, and most edd. do so likewise, except Hanmer whom we follow. Ll. 221, 223 are certainly verse, and so would l. 222 be if the word 'master' or 'Tranio' was omitted. The speech has probably been abbreviated, v. last note but one.

231. *becomes,* F. 'becomes:'

237–42. *So could I...Lucentio* F. prints as prose: Capell first arranged as verse, thus revealing a patch of the old (? pre-Shakespearian) rhyming doggerel, traces of which we have found in *Errors,* 3. 1. 11–83 (cf. p. 77), *L.L.L.* 4. 2. 22–35, etc. and which crop up again at ll. 245, 246 below.

242. *your master* (F 2) F. 'you maſter'

243. broken line.

245–46. *To make one...weighty* Thus F. prints.

Pope read as prose and all edd. have followed him; but the lines are rhyme-doggerel again.

246. S.D. F. 'Exeunt. The Preſenters aboue ſpeakes.' The Presenter, who was a common figure on the Eliz. stage though rarely found in Shakespeare except in mockery as in the case of Quince (v. *M.N.D.* 5. 1. 107 S.D., 126–50, notes), was strictly speaking one who 'presented' a play, an act, or a scene, by explaining what was about to take place. He stood outside the plot and commented upon it; in this last sense Sly and the rest were 'presenters' also.

252. S.D. F. 'They ſit and marke.' After this promise of continued attention F. tells us nothing more of Sly and his party, and much speculation has been raised to account for their disappearance, especially seeing that in *A Shrew* the presenters go on with their comments until the very end of the play (cf. pp. xvii, 123–24). We suggest that the dropping of the Sly business at this point was due to purely theatrical exigencies and not to any action by Shakespeare; in other words, that *The Shrew*, like *A Shrew*, originally continued Sly until the end of the play. It has been supposed (v. Bond, p. 33) that the appearance of the Pedant (5. 1. 16) at 'the window' caused the removal of Sly; but the explanation is not adequate, seeing that such a window might be over one of the side-doors and not in the gallery at all (v. Chambers, *Eliz. Stage*, iii. 119–20). The free use of the gallery would be a help in 4. 1., and we have arranged the scene on those lines; but the bridal chamber need not necessarily be upstairs. On the whole, the real cause was probably economy in man-power. To keep three players up in the gallery throughout the play, speaking only occasionally and never able to help out the main action by doubling, would have seemed a crime to any practical stage-manager of the period, unless he were very rich in actors. That the cast for the F. text was none too strong is suggested

by the appearance of Hortensio in 4. 3. (v. note 4. 1. 141), while 4. 1. with Curtis and five other speaking servants, to say nothing of supers, made great demands upon the company.

1. 2.

S.D. F. 'Enter Petruchio, and his man Grumio.'

2. *Padua*, F. 'Padua;'

13. F. prints in two lines thus: 'My Mr. is growne quarrelſome:/I ſhould knocke you firſt,'

17. S.D. F. 'He rings him by the eares'

18. *masters* (Theobald) F. 'miſtris' This misprint recurs twice in this text (5. 1. 6, 51), and its converse is found in *M.V.* 4. 1. 51 (where in a spirit of over-zealous conservatism we have erroneously read 'Master'). The probable explanation of the error is the presence in the copy of the contracted form 'Mrs' for 'masters.' Cf. 'Mr.' (Master) in note l. 13 above.

19. S.D. F. 'Enter Hortenſio.'

24. *Con tutto* etc. (Theobald) F. 'Contutti le core bene trobatto.' v. G.

25. *ben* (F2) F. 'bene' *molto honorato signor* (Theobald) F. 'multo honorata ſignior' v. G. 'Alla nostra casa ben venuto.'

31. *sir: well*, F. 'ſir. Well,'

32–3. *two and thirty, a pip out* v. G.
pip F. 'peepe'

34–5. *Whom would...the worst* F. prints as prose, with the rest of the speech. These rhyming couplets embedded in prose strongly suggest revision.

36. *A senseless villain!* Antipholus of Ephesus concludes his thwacking of Dromio with the same expression (*Errors*, 4. 4. 23), and the episodes are in other respects similar.

39–42. *Knock at the gate* etc. Capell attempted to arrange these as four lines of verse, and the fact that

And come you now with 'knocking at the gate'?

forms an indubitable verse-line suggests that the whole speech was originally verse.

45. *this'* F. 'this' i.e. this is. Cf. *Meas.* 5. 1. 130.

'twixt F. '*twixr*' Cf. notes 4. 2. 10, 29. The *r* and *t* boxes in the compositor's case have clearly got mixed.

49–51. *Such wind...grows* Cf. *Two Gent.* 1. 1. 2–8.

51. *grows. But in a few,* F. 'growes but in a few.'

53. *Antonio* So F. here and at 2. 1. 68. The usual F. sp. is 'Anthonio'

55. *Haply* (Malone) F. 'Happily' Cf. 4. 4. 54.

59, 63. *wish* v. G.

66. *wife—* F. 'wife:'

67. *burthen* i.e. the musical accompaniment which controls the dancer's steps.

69–70. *Sibyl...Xanthippe* (F2) F. 'Sibell...Zentippe' For 'Sibyl' v. G. 70. *worse,* F. 'worſe:'

72. *me, were* F. 'me. Were' *she as* (F2) F. 'ſhe is as'

78. *aglet-baby* v. G. Nashe twice uses the word 'aglet' (McKerrow, *Nashe,* i. 166, 21; ii. 227, 26) which is not found elsewhere in Shakespeare. We find it hard to withstand the suspicion that Nashe had something to do with the parts of Grumio and Biondello in this text. Cf. note 3. 2. 43–61.

79–80. *diseases...horses* It is Biondello who at 3. 2. 49–55 shows himself the authority on equine disorders.

86. *gentlewoman.* So F. 108–9. *upon him.* So F.

111. *rope-tricks.* So F. Bond comments: 'Doubtless this is Grumio's mistake for "rhetoric," to which "figure" is appropriate; but remembering the tenor of those remarks of Mercutio which the nurse characterises as "ropery" (*Rom.* 2. 4. 154) I trace in "rope-tricks" a *double entendre* expressing a situation in which abuse would be unusual, and believe we have similar coarse allusions in the two following lines.' If owing to a foul case (cf. note l. 45 above) 'rope' were a

misprint for 'tope' (= tup), we should get much the same meaning.

119. *from me and other* (Capell) F. 'from me. Other'

132. *Well seen* i.e. well taught. A common expression, but not found elsewhere in Shakespeare.

137. S.D. F. 'Enter Gremio and Lucentio disguised.'—at l. 135.

139. *love.* So F.

140. *Petruchio, stand by a while.* Clark and Wright conj. that the 'Petruchio' here should be a speech-heading.

141. *A proper stripling* etc. Grumio is, of course, referring to Gremio the pantaloon.

142. *the note* i.e. the list of books which Lucentio proposes to take with him.

144. *at any hand* = in any case.

149. *them* i.e. the books.

151. *they go* (Rowe) F. 'they go to' Cf. pp. 97–8.

161. *Hortensio.* So F.

170. *help me* (Rowe) F. 'helpe one' 178. *either.* So F.

180. *Upon agreement* etc. Cf. ll. 212–13 below. The two passages taken together suggest that Hortensio and Petruchio have plotted to make something out of the old 'woodcock'; but the point is not explicit and is never followed up.

188. *Antonio's* (Rowe) F. 'Butonios'—an instance of compositor's 'wrong box.'

191. *Sir, such a life* (Capell) F. 'Oh sir, such a life' The extra-metrical 'Oh' of the F. is probably derived from the last syllable of the speech-heading 'Gremi-o.' Cf. for other examples *L.L.L.* 2. 1. 211, 3. 1. 142, 4. 3. 279, 285 (notes).

204. *trumpets'* (Capell) F. 'trumpets'

206. *to hear* Hanmer read 'to th'ear,' an attractive emendation, involving no graphical difficulties, since Shakespeare would probably write 'thear' as one word,

while *th* and *h* were liable to confusion in English script.

208. *fear boys with bugs* v. G. 'fear,' 'bug.' Cf. 3 *Hen. VI*, 5. 2. 2 'Warwick was a bug that feared us all.'

211. *ours* (Theobald) F. 'yours'

215. S.D. F. 'Enter Tranio braue, and Biondello.'

216–18. *Gentlemen, God save you* etc. F. and most edd. print these lines as verse; Pope printed them as prose. The feeble rhyme 'way-Minola' suggests an outcrop of the basic rhyme-doggerel, which is undoubtedly found a few lines further on (ll. 221–28).

219. *He that has* etc. 'Biondello is obviously playing a prearranged part' (Bond).

221. *her too?* (Tyrwhitt) F. 'her to—' Tyrwhitt is assuredly right. The spellings 'to' and 'too' are interchangeable in Shakespearian texts, and the F. dash only denotes the bewilderment of the compositor. Gremio's remark is perfectly natural: 'Why, you're not thinking of her too?' he exclaims, his mind full of Bianca, while Tranio's retort follows up, of course, what he has just said to Biondello.

231. *know* F. 'kno'—presumably as an eye-rhyme to 'Gremio.'

235. *patience.* So F. 239. *for one.* So F.

240. *Leda's daughter* i.e. Helen. Cf. Marlowe (*Dr Faustus*, sc. xiii. 91) 'Was this the face that launched a thousand ships?'

245. *prove a jade* i.e. soon tire. v. G. 'jade.'

256. *hearken for* v. G. 'hearken.'

259. *wed.* So F.

263. *feat* (Rowe) F. 'ſeeke' The letters *k* and *t* in English script were not unlike if carelessly formed. Cf. Sh.Hand, plates v and vi, and 'bleake' for 'bleat' (*M.V.* 4. 1. 74), 'kyth' for 'tithe' (*Ham.* 3. 4. 97), etc.

264. *elder,* F. 'elder:'

272. *contrive* v. G.

278. *ben venuto* (F 2) F. 'Been venuto' v. G. Hortensio means he will be Petruchio's host.

S.D. F. 'Exeunt.'

2. 1.

S.D. F. 'Enter Katherina and Bianca.' F. gives neither act nor scene heading here; cf. *Acts and Scenes*, p. 127.

3. *gauds* (Theobald) F. 'goods' Cf. p. 103.

8. *charge thee* (F 2) F. 'charge' Cf. pp. 97–8.

17. *fair* i.e. fine.

18. *envy* usually accented on the 2nd syllable; v. G.

22. S.D. F. 'Strikes her/Enter Baptiſta.'

25. *with her.* So F.

29. S.D. F. 'Flies after Bianca'

30. S.D. F. 'Exit.'

33–4. *dance bare-foot...lead apes in hell* both proverbial occupations of old-maidhood. Cf. *Ado*, 2. 1. 37, and G.

36. S.D. F. gives no 'exit' for Katharina.

38. S.D. F. 'Enter Gremio, Lucentio, in the habit of a meane man, Petruchio with Tranio, with his boy bearing a Lute and Bookes.' The awkward 'with Tranio with his boy' shows that Hortensio has been omitted by the transcriber or compositor. The 'boy' is of course Biondello. The expression 'meane man' seems to be derived from 1. 1. 204, v. note.

42–3. *And you, good sir* etc. F. prints as prose; Capell first arranged as verse.

56–8. *Cunning in music...not ignorant* This scene, with its later reference to 'Greek, Latin, and other languages' (l. 81), is suggestive on the subject of the kind of education given to the daughters of well-to-do parents at this period, a matter upon which we have little direct evidence. 'Mathematics' is perhaps the most surprising of the subjects mentioned.

60. *Licio* (F 2) F. 'Litio'

61. *sake*. So F.

68. *Antonio's* v. note 1. 2. 53.

71–3. *Saving your tale...forward.* F. prints as prose and it is doubtful whether Steevens was well-advised in arranging it as verse, though all mod. edd. have followed him. Capell attempted a slightly different arrangement.

74–87. *O, pardon me* etc. F. prints Petruchio's speech as prose, Grumio's and Baptista's as verse. Rowe first detected the 'doing-wooing' rhyme and Pope arranged the rest as prose. The mixture of verse and prose, together with the line-arrangement of the whole passage ll. 71–87, suggests revision.

75–6. *sir;* F. 'ſir.' *wooing./Neighbour,* (Theobald) F. 'wooing neighbors:'

78. *any,* (Pope) F. 'any:'

79. *unto you* (Capell) F. 'vnto' Cf. pp. 97–8.

80–1. *cunning in Greek, Latin* etc. Cf. 'Greek and Latin books' l. 100 below and note ll. 56–8 above.

82. *Cambio* The word means 'exchange'; it is found again in Kyd's *Soliman and Perseda,* 2. 2. 17.

90. *a suitor* F. 'aſ utor'

93. *sister.* So F. 97. *rest.* So F.

98. *daughters* F. 'daughters:'

101. *great.* F. 'great:'

108. S.D. F. 'Enter a Seruant.'

109. *both* Capell added the words 'from me' Cf. pp. 97–8.

112. *And then to dinner* The dinner presumably is supposed to take place after the 'exeunt' at l. 168.

124. *widowhood* v. G.

130. *father* This is a nice touch; assuredly Petruchio is 'marvellous forward.'

133. *fury.* So F.

141. *shake* (F 2) F. 'ſhakes'

S.D. F. 'Enter Hortenſio with his head broke.'

146. *hold with her* i.e. will not break in her hands.

156. *As on a pillory* v. G. 'pillory.'

163. *discomfited.* So F.

168. *do.* So F. *I will* (Rowe) F. 'Ile'

S.D. F. 'Exit. Manet Petruchio'—at l. 167.

169 et seq. Amid much in this play of doubtful authorship, a speech like this has the unmistakable Shakespearian ring.

172–73. *Say that she frown...washed with dew* Hickson (v. pp. 122–23) notes that the reporter responsible for the material for *A Shrew* transfers this to 4. 5., and puts it into Katharine's mouth as part of her address to the Duke of Cestus (=Vincentio) whom she describes as a fair lovely lady

> As glorious as the morning wa∫ht with dew.

Roses 'washed with dew' are intelligible, but what is a morning in this kind?

180. *married.* So F.

181. *speak.* So F.

S.D. F. 'Enter Katerina.'

182–271. *Good morrow, Kate* etc. This word-combat, full of indelicate quibbles, is from the same mint as those which occupy so much space in *L.L.L.*, and is evidently Shakespeare's.

186. *bonny* (F4) F. 'bony' v. G.

188. *Kate Hall* In Aug. 1591 the queen's harbinger was allowed payment "for making ready a dining-house at Katharine Hall," one of the places in the South of England at which Elizabeth stopped on a summer progress which included visits to Cowdray, the house of Southampton's grandfather, and Titchfield, the house of Southampton himself (Stopes, *Life of Southampton*, p. 45).

189. *all cates* (Pope) F. 'all Kates'

195. *in good time!* i.e. forsooth! v. G. 'time.'

201. *such a jade* (S. Walker) F. 'ſuch Iade' Cf. pp. 97–8. A jade (v. G.) is a horse that soon tires. The text, therefore, as it stands is capable of an obvious, if indelicate, interpretation, which renders quite unnecessary the various emendations offered for 'Iade' by edd. A jade might be of either sex.

204. *Too light...catch* 'too quick for a rustic wit like yours' (Bond).

205. *as heavy as my weight should be* Is it possible that there is some reference to catch-weights in horse-racing here?

206. *should—buzz!* F. 'ſhould: buzze.' Almost the only piece of dramatic punctuation in this text. 'Buzz' (v. G.) is of course a quibble on 'bee' (be), cf. *Ham.* 2. 2. 412. Petruchio's hint is that scandal has another story to tell of Katharine's lightness.

208. *Ay, for a turtle,* etc. i.e. the fool will take me for a faithful wife, as the turtle-dove swallows the cockchafer (v. G. 'buzzard'). That this is the quibble intended is borne out by the reference to 'wasp,' another kind of buzzard or buzzing insect.

214. *In his tail* / *In his tongue* } The two replies should be spoken simultaneously.

215. *tales* So F. Katharine is of course quibbling upon 'tails,' but it is unnecessary to read this as Rowe and all subsequent edd. have done.

217. *gentleman—* F. 'Gentleman,'

S.D. F. 'ſhe ſtrikes him'

219. *loose your arms* F. makes no difference in sp. between 'lose' and 'loose': nor was there probably any in 16th century pronunciation. The quibble, a frequent one with Shakespeare, is obvious if Petruchio has her tightly held.

221. *no arms* A coat of arms was the sine qua non of a gentleman at this period. Aspiring candidates for the rank purchased such coats from the College of Heralds, one of them being the poet's father, John Shakespeare,

who applied for a coat in 1596 and received it in 1599. (Lee, *Life*, pp. 281–87.)

222. *in thy books* to be in the herald's books was tantamount to becoming a gentleman. v. also G. 'books.'

225. *craven* a fighting-cock that is not game, v. G.

227. *crab* The word means both 'wild apple' and 'cross-grained person.'

232. *too young for you* i.e. too strong for you. Cf. *Ado*, 5. 1. 118.

235. *chafe* Another quibble, v. G.

240. *flowers*. So F.

241. *askance* F. 'a ſconce' v. G.

251. *whom thou keep'st command* i.e. order your own servants about, not me.

259. *keep you warm* Proverbial; cf. *Ado*, 1. 1. 63–4 'if he have wit enough to keep himself warm.' Katharine implies that Petruchio has just this amount and no more.

270. *wild Kate* with a quibble of course upon 'wild-cat.'

271. *Kates* Theobald conj. 'cats'

S.D. F. 'Enter Baptiſta, Gremio, Trayno.'—at l. 268.

288. *a second Grissel* The story of Griselda, 'the flour of wyfly pacience,' is first told in Boccaccio's *Decameron*, whence Chaucer borrowed it for his *Clerkes Tale*.

294. *good night* F. 'godnight' 298. *company*. So F.

303. *love*. So F.

317. S.D. F. 'Exit Petruchio and Katherine.' Petruchio had been careful to get a hold upon her, as ll. 307, 311 show, so that the kiss might be properly administered.

321. *fretting* v. G. Tranio quibbles.

323. *quiet in* (Rowe) F. 'quiet me'—'inne' taken for 'me' Cf. 4. 2. 71 (note).

324. *a quiet catch* 'properly of something good but unobserved' (Bond); cf. 'a great catch' *Troil.* 2. 1. 110.

332. *Skipper* v. G.

337. broken line.

have Bianca's (F2) F. 'haue my Biancas loue' The metrically disturbing 'my' may have been caught from the line above.

347. *needle work,* F. 'needle worke:'

348. *belong* (Rowe) F. 'belongs'

350. *to the pail* v. G. 'pail.' 364. *pinched* v. G.

368. *Marseilles'* F. 'Marcellus' F2 'Marsellis' v. p. 103.

378. *out-vied* v. G. 'vie.'

381. *own—else, you must pardon me,* F. 'owne, elſe you muſt pardon me:'

385–86. *Well, gentlemen...know* F. divides 'Well ...reſolu'd,/On ſonday...know' It looks as if there has been some adaptation here.

390. broken line.

391. S.D. F. 'Exit.'

393. *gamester* 'Perhaps alluding to the pretended Lucentio's having before talked of out-vying him' (Malone); v. G. 'vie.' Malone's interpretation is supported by l. 398 below.

395. *Set foot under thy table* 'live as your pensioner' (Bond).

396. S.D. F. 'Exit.'

398. *faced it with a card of ten* brazened it out, v. G. 'card of ten.'

404. S.D. F. 'Exit.'

3. 1.

F. heads the scene 'Actus Tertia.' S.D. F. 'Enter Lucentio, Hortentio, and Bianca.' *Hortensio...fingering* We base our S.D. on ll. 2–3 of the scene which are a clear reference to 2. 1. 150.

4. *But, wrangling pedant,* etc. Theobald inserted 'She is a shrew' at the beginning of this line. The guess is as good as any. Possibly there has been some kind of cut here.

9. *Preposterous* The word is used literally.

14. *serve in* Lucentio speaks of music as if it were some after-dinner trifle.

18. *breeching scholar* v. G.

21. *strife,* F. 'ſtrife:' *down:* F. 'downe,'—transposed pointing.

24. *in tune* Lucentio takes this in the sense of 'in a good temper,' v. G. 'tune.'

28–9. *Hic ibat* etc. The passage is from Ovid (*Her.* i. 33) and runs in English 'Here ran the river Simois; here is the Sigeian land; here stood the lofty palace of old Priam.' Theobald read 'Hac ibat' etc., following the original.

28, 33, 42. *Sigeia* (F 2) F. 'ſigeria'

30. *Conster* the old form of 'construe.'

36. *pantaloon* Cf. 1. 1. 47 S.D. and v. G.

40. *Spit in the hole* To spit into the sound-hole in the lute would not help to tune it, but to spit was a common action before making a second attempt; cf. *A.Y.L.* 4. 1. 72–3 'very good orators, when they are out, they will spit.'

43. *steterat* (F 2) F. 'ſtaterat'

46–60. For the F. distribution of speeches here v. pp. 101–102.

48. *How fiery* etc. A halting line.

50. *Pedascule* 'He should have said "Didascule," but thinking this too honourable, he coins the word "Pedascule" in imitation of it from "pedant"' (Warburton), upon which Steevens comments, 'I believe it is no coinage of Shakespeare's; it is more probable that it lay in his way and he found it.' v. G.

yet. F. 'yet:'—pointing based on the mistaken notion that the speech includes the line following.

52–3. *Æacides/Was Ajax* etc. 'The pedigree...is properly made out, and might have been taken from Golding's version of Ovid's *Metamorphoses*, xiii' (Steevens).

56. *Licio* (Rowe) F. 'Litio'

57. *Good master* So F. Rowe and all subsequent edd. until Bond read 'Good masters.' Bond comments: 'She is addressing Hortensio, who alone has reason to be displeased; and "pleasant with you both" stretches her apology to cover Lucentio's chaff, and her laughter at it.' The restoration of the text adds a new touch to the coquette's character.

67. *gamut* F. 'gamoth' At ll. 71, 72, 73, 79 the sp. is 'gamouth'; v. G.

73. *accord* i.e. harmony. Hortensio hints at love's harmony. Cf. G. 'ground.'

75. *B mi* (Pope) F. 'Beeme'

77. *clef* F. 'Cliffe' *one clef, two notes have I* Bond interprets 'one clef' as Love and 'two notes' as Hortensio-Licio's dual personality.

81. *change* (F2) F. 'charge'—an *n* : *r* misprint, v. Ham. Sp. and Misp. p. 41.

odd (Theobald) F. 'old'—an *l* : *d* misprint, v. Ham. Sp. and Misp. p. 45.

S.D. F. 'Enter a Meſſenger.'

82. *Mistress*, etc. F. heads this, the only speech of the servant, 'Nicke,' which Steevens interpreted Nicholas Tooley, who appears in the list of 'The names of the Principall Actors' at the beginning of the Folio. Cf. pp. 116–17.

85, 86. S.D. F. gives no 'exit' either for Bianca or Lucentio.

90. *stale*, F. 'ſtale:' Bianca is the falcon stooping to a false lure; v. G. 'stale' (ii).

91. *ranging* v. G. 'range.'

92. S.D. F. 'Exit.'

3.2.

S.D. F. 'Enter Baptifta, Gremio, Tranio, Katherine, Bianca, and others, attendants.'

10. *full of spleen* v. G. 'spleen.'

13. *behaviour:* F. 'behauiour,' 14. *man,* F. 'man;'—transposed pointing.

16. *Make feast, invite friends,* F. 'Make friends, inuite,' Dyce, citing 2. 1. 309 'Provide the feast, father, and bid the guests,' proposed 'Make feasts, invite friends.' If 'feast' be read for 'feasts,' this seems the best emendation among a host of guesses. The compositor's, or transcriber's, eye perhaps travelled prematurely from 'feast' to 'friends' in his copy, and the rest would follow.

26. S.D. F. 'Exit weeping.'

28. *a saint* (F2) F. 'a very saint' The 'very' is an obvious interpolation and there is no more reason for retaining it in this line than there is for refusing to insert 'thy' in the next.

29. *thy impatient* (F2) F. 'impatient'

S.D. F. 'Enter Biondello.'

30. *such old news* (Collier) F. 'fuch newes' Baptista's question in reply shows that the word 'old' has been omitted. Rowe read 'old news and such news,' Capell 'news, old news, and such news,' but Collier's reading seems the simplest and most natural. This makes the third bad misprint in three consecutive lines; cf. pp. 97–8.

31. *heard of!* F. 'heard of,'

33. *hear* (F2) F. 'heard'

43–61. Tennyson told Furnivall in 1874 that this famous and racy description of Petruchio's get-up 'has such a rollicking Rabelaisian comic swing about it, that I cannot but suspect it to be genuine Shakspere' (New Shak. Soc. *Trans.* 1874, pt. i. 105). But had Tennyson read Nashe, whose work was not made available to modern readers until Grosart's edition of 1883? Tennyson's words 'a rollicking Rabelaisian comic swing' exactly express the quality of his style and Nashe especially delighted in descriptions of costume of a miserly or beggarly character. Alongside with that of Petruchio and Grumio in the text may be set this of Greediness and his Dame Niggardize from *Pierce Penilesse* (McKerrow, i. 166–67):

In the inner part of this vgly habitation stands Greedinesse, prepared to deuoure all that enter, attyred in a Capouch of written parchment, buttond downe before with Lapels of wax, and lined with sheepes fels for warmenes: his Cappe furd with cats skins, after the Muscouie fashion, and all to be tasseld with Angle-hookes, in stead of Aglets, ready to catch hold of all those to whom he shewes any humblenes: for his breeches, they were made of the lists of broad cloaths, which he had by letters pattents assured him and his heyres...and bumbasted they were, like Beerebarrels, with statute Marchants and forfeitures. But of al, his shooes were the strangest, which being nothing els but a couple of crab shels, were toothd at the tooes with two sharp sixpennie nailes, that digd vp euery dunghil they came by for gould....On the other side, Dame Niggardize his wife, in a sedge rug kirtle, that had beene a mat time out of minde, a course hempen raile about her shoulders, borrowed of the one end of a hop-bag, an apron made of Almanackes out of date (such as stand vpon Screens, or on the backside of a dore in a Chandlers shop), and an old wiues pudding pan on her head, thrumd with the parings of her nailes.

Apart from other things, the prose-rhythm of the two passages seems very similar.

44. *jerkin;* F. 'ierkin,'

45. *boots...candle-cases* i.e. boots too old for wear, used as receptacles for candle-ends.

48–9. *with an old mothy...hipped besides* (Rann) F. 'his horſe hip'd with an olde mothy ſaddle, and ſtirrops of no kindred: beſides'—which makes nonsense. The words 'with an old mothy saddle, and stirrups of no kindred' would take up about a line of MS.

Suppose the transcriber to have omitted the line accidentally, to have added it in the margin later, but with such insufficient indication of its rightful position that the compositor inserted it incorrectly, and the mistake would be explained.

50. *mose in the chine* That the phrase means to suffer from the glanders is not really in doubt, but the word 'mose' which is not found elsewhere is almost certainly corrupt. To 'mourn of (or 'on') the chine' is the usual form of the expression, but since 'pose' was also a form of glanders this may be the word intended, the *p* being converted to *m* by the transcriber's inadvertence or the compositor's 'foul case.'

54. *bots, swayed* (Hanmer) F. 'Bots, Waid'—possibly *ſw* read as *W*; but v. p. 103.

55. *near-legged before* i.e. standing with the fore-legs close together. As this is a virtue in a horse, it is clear that what the author intended to write was 'near-legged behind.'

58. *new-repaired* (S. Walker) F. 'now repaired'—an *o* : *e* misprint. The F. reading would denote a single operation, while the whole point of the thing is the number of times the head-stall had been repaired, each occasion being marked by a new knot.

66–7. *the humour of forty fancies* 'Some ballad or drollery' (Warburton), 'some fantastical ornament comprising the humour of forty fancies' (Malone), and there are many other suggestions. In short, no one knows what it means.

80–84. F. prints this jingle as prose. Collier first arranged it as five lines of verse.

84. *many* with a quibble upon 'meiny'

S.D. F. 'Enter Petruchio and Grumio.'

87. *you halt not* He refers to Petruchio's boisterous manner of approach.

87–8. *Not so...wish you were* F. prints this in one line.

89. *Were it not better* (Keightley) F. 'Were it better' The F. reading gives no sense, and this text is full of little omissions; cf. pp. 97–8.

121. *lovely* i.e. loving. N.B. Not found elsewhere in Shakespeare in this sense, though frequent in Lyly.

S.D. F. 'Exit.'

125. S.D. F. 'Exit.' Some intervening scene or episode seems to have been excised here. Note (1) the talk between Tranio and Lucentio (ll. 126–46) allows just 20 lines for Petruchio to greet Katharine, carry her off to church, and go through the marriage-ceremony—truly the hastiest wedding in the whole Shakespearian canon; (2) Tranio's words (ll. 122–24) imply that he follows Baptista, to use his influence with Petruchio for more seemly attire—yet he stays behind; (3) his words (ll. 126 et sqq.) open with an abruptness quite in keeping with the beginning of a scene but absurd here. He is obviously in the middle of a conversation with Lucentio, yet he was talking to Baptista one line earlier; (4) the F. text provides no entry for Lucentio at the head of 3. 2.; (5) the continuity of the scene creates the one serious difficulty in the setting of this play; cf. 1. 1. head-note.

126. *But to her love* (Grant White) F. 'But ſir, Loue' Grant White's is the best of a number of guesses and has been accepted by most edd. Bond suggests that 'sir' was 'obviously an aural error for "to her"'; cf. p. 103.

128. *As I before* (Pope) F. 'As before'

137. *narrowly*, F. 'narrowly:'

138. *steal our marriage* Cf. *Rom.* 5. 3. 233 'their stol'n marriage-day.'

145. *Licio* (Rowe) F. 'Litio'

146. S.D. F. 'Enter Gremio.'

151. *grumbling* (F 2) F. 'grumlling'

158. *gogs-wouns* F. 'goggs woones' v. G.

164. *arose* (Steevens) F. 'roſe' Cf. pp. 97–8.

165–81. *Trembled and shook* etc. F. prints this whole speech as prose. Possibly it was originally crowded into the foot or margin of a foolscap page. It is of course all pure Shakespeare.

170. *muscadel* 'At the conclusion of the [marriage] service a cup of muscadel with cakes or sops in it was drunk by the bride, the bridegroom, and the company' (Sh.Eng. ii. 147). Petruchio left none for bride or company.

181. *Hark, hark* etc. A short line.

S.D. F. 'Muſicke playes./Enter Petruchio, Kate, Bianca, Hortenſio, Baptiſta.'

197. *Let me entreat you*. F. heads this 'Gra.' (for 'Gre.').

202. *my horse* 'Horse, in our author's time, was used in the plural' (Malone).

203–204. *the oats have eaten the horses* i.e. they are full-up with oats, and therefore very 'ready.' Possibly Grumio added point to the jest by pronouncing 'oats' as 'aits,' a 16th century variant—thus: 'the aits have aten the horses.'

205. *Nay, then,* A broken line like this at the beginning of the speech suggests revision.

207. *nor to-morrow, till I please* F. 'nor to morrow, not till I pleaſe' S. Walker conj. 'nor to-morrow, not till please'; F4, which many follow, gives 'tomorrow, nor till I please.' We suppose that the transcriber here, as so often elsewhere (v. pp. 97–8) has added a 'not,' confused by the preceding 'not...no, nor.'

226. *Nay, look not big* etc. Petruchio's cue is to say this angrily to those who stand about him, while pretending not to see that Katharine suits the action to his words.

237. S.D. F. 'Exeunt P. Ka.'

243. *Kated* i.e. caught the Kate-complaint.

250. S.D. F. 'Exeunt.'

4. 1.

S.D. F. 'Enter Grumio.' F. gives the heading 'Actus Quartus' at the beginning of 4. 3. (q.v.).

6. *a little pot, and soon hot* proverbial. Steevens quotes Day's *Isle of Gulls*, 1606, 'Though I be but a little pot, I shall be as soon hot as another.' Grumio refers, of course, to his size; cf. 'a taller man than I' (l. 10), and 'three-inch fool' (l. 24) and p. 119.

hot, F. 'hot;'

10. *considering the weather* This scene, we may suppose, was written for a performance in winter-time during a period of intense cold.

11. S.D. F. 'Enter Curtis.' Cf. p. 118.

17–18. *fire, fire, cast on no water* referring to the well-known catch

Scotland's burning, Scotland's burning,
See yonder! See yonder!
Fire, fire! Fire, fire!
Cast on more water.

24. *I am no beast* By naming himself the third of the tamed Grumio has called himself a beast, and Curtis, his 'fellow,' by implication one likewise.

25. *thy horn* the eternal jest on cuckoldry, of which the Elizabethans never tired.

33. *Do thy duty* etc. Proverbial once more—'do thy duty and take thy due,' v. G. 'duty.'

38. *Jack boy! ho boy!* The beginning of another catch; the first two lines are thus given in Ravenscroft's *Pammelia* (1609):

Jacke boy, ho boy, Newes:
The cat is in the well.

Possibly the reference to the cat might link the catch in the minds of the audience with Kate the shrew.

39. *thou wilt* (F2) F. 'wilt thou' Badham conj. 'will thaw.'

40. *cony-catching* i.e. evasion, v. G. Curtis refers quibblingly to Grumio's love of catches.

44. *their white* (F 3) F. 'the white'

46. *jacks...jills* v. G.

the carpets laid 'In our author's time it was customary to cover tables with carpets. Floors, as appears from the present passage and others, were strewed with rushes' (Malone).

58. *This is* (Rowe) F. 'This 'tis'

63–5. *Both of one horse* etc. There seems to be some indelicate jest here.

81–2. It is noteworthy that the names given in the verse (ll. 121–25) do not entirely correspond with this prose list.

82. *sleekly* F. 'ſlickely'

83. *blue coats* Dark blue was the usual colour of servants' dress, as it still is, while the fashion has been inherited by those servants of John Citizen, the police and the postmen.

84. *knit;* F. 'knit,'

93. *calls* 2nd pers. sing. pres.; cf. *Temp.* 1. 2. 334 (note).

96. S.D. F. 'Enter foure or fiue ſeruingmen.'

100. F. heads this 'Nick' (=Nicholas); v. pp. 116–17.

108. S.D. F. 'Enter Petruchio and Kate.'

109. *at the door* (Capell) F. 'at doore' Cf. pp. 97–8.

118. *peasant swain* (Rowe) F. 'pezant, ſwain'

malt-horse drudge Cf. *Every Man in his Humour* (1616), 1. 5. 89 'no more judgement than a malt-horse.'

121–27. *Nathaniel's coat* etc. Not only do the servants' names vary from those given in the prose above (ll. 81–2 note), but Grumio's excuses sort oddly with the emphatic assurances by Curtis that the servants are 'all ready and all things neat.' It is moreover strange to find Grumio speaking blank verse.

122. *Gabriel's pumps* v. pp. 114, 118.

128. S.D. F. 'Ex. Ser.'

129. *Where is the life that late I led* The first line of a lost ballad, 'peculiarly suited to Petruchio's present situation: for it appears to have been descriptive of the state of a lover who has newly resigned his freedom' (Malone). Malone's statement is based upon the title to a 'reply' to the ballad which appears in Clement Robinson's *Handeful of Pleasant Delites*, 1584.

130. *Where are those* This may be merely one of Petruchio's outbursts against the servants, or (as Theobald thought) the beginning of the second line of the ballad.

132. *Food, food, food, food!* F. 'Soud, ſoud, ſoud, ſoud.' The F. nonsense has given rise to the usual variety of strained explanations, and Onions (*Shakespeare Glossary*) throws up the sponge with the words 'interjection of doubtful import.' Yet 'food' (as 'foud,' a quite possible MS sp. of the 16th century, v. Wyld, *Hist. Mod. Colloquial English*, p. 235) might easily be misprinted as 'ſoud,' and 'food' is the interjection (of no doubtful import) which is most appropriate in Petruchio's mouth at this juncture.

S.D. F. 'Enter ſeruants with ſupper.'

135–36. *It was a friar* etc. Another fragment of a lost ballad.

139. S.D. F. 'Enter one with water.' Edd. have all ignored the F. position of this S.D., postponing the entry of the water until l. 143 when Petruchio calls a second time for it. But the whole point of the scene is that the service of Petruchio's house is excellent, only the master takes everything amiss, his object being to give the shrew a drastically conceived object-lesson of the effects of choler.

141. *my cousin Ferdinand* The servant goes out, but Ferdinand never appears and in the next Petruchio scene Hortensio oddly turns up, apparently in Ferdinand's place. Cf. p. 125.

S.D. F. gives no 'exit' for the servant.

146. *Patience, I pray you* etc. That Katharine is beginning to enjoin patience is a good symptom.

157. S.D. *he chases them* etc. This S.D. is required by (*a*) Petruchio's words 'I'll be with you straight' i.e. I'll be after you!, and (*b*) the F. S.D. at l. 168 'Enter Seruants ſeuerally.' On the other hand, it is clear from ll. 172–77 that in the received text Curtis, who is a kind of steward, is intended to remain behind to escort the bridal pair to their chamber. But cf. note l. 170 S.D. below.

165. *over-roasted flesh* Marshall aptly cites *Err.* 2. 2. 54–62 where the same effects are attributed to eating 'dry meat.'

168. S.D. F. 'Exeunt./Enter Seruants ſeuerally.'

170. S.D. F. 'Enter Curtis a Seruant.' Considering that Curtis has been on for most of the scene the F. description 'a Seruant' is oddly superfluous. Is it possible that this was Curtis' first entry in the original play, and that the prose dialogue between Grumio and Curtis, which we noticed suited awkwardly with what followed (v. note ll. 121–27 above), was written later? Curtis, it may be remarked, is not mentioned at Petruchio's entry, despite his obvious standing in the household. Cf. note 4. 4. 17 S.D.

172–77. *In her chamber* etc. F. prints the whole speech as prose; this, taken with the fact that the speech begins with a scrap of prose, suggests revision and re-copying.

177. S.D. F. 'Enter Petruchio.' F. gives no 'exeunt' for the servants.

180–86. *My falcon* etc. This falcon passage, which bears the Shakespearian hall-mark, will be more readily followed if it be glossed in a single note. Thus *sharp* = famished; *stoop* = fly to the lure; *lure* = a kind of leather frame carried by the falconer and garnished with pieces of meat; *man a haggard* = tame a wild hawk;

watch = prevent the hawk from sleeping; *kite* = falcon (with a possible quibble upon 'Kate'); *bate and beat* = flutter and flap the wings impatiently. See G. for further information.

185. *these kites* i.e. those kites. Shakespeare often uses 'these' to denote some topical or well-known object or person; cf. *Rom.* 1. 1. 236 'these happy masks.'

187. *eat;* F. 'eate.'

193. *intend* i.e. pretend.

201. S.D. F. 'Exit.'

4. 2.

S.D. F. 'Enter Tranio and Hortenſio:' On the stage Bianca and Lucentio would probably be discovered by the drawing aside of the curtains.

1–5. This looks like adapter's patch-work: the first and fourth lines are prose. Prose recurs again in ll. 11–14, yet the rest of the scene is smooth if insipid verse.

4–8. *Sir, to satisfy* etc. F. wrongly distributes the speeches in this passage, v. pp. 101–102.

5. F. here gives S.D. 'Enter Bianca.' See head-note above and p. 103.

7. *you? first* F. 'you firſt'

8. *I read...Love* F. punctuates 'I reade, that I profeſſe the Art to loue.' *the Art to Love* F. 'the Art to loue' i.e. Ovid's *Ars Amandi.*

10. *prove* F. 'ptoue' Cf. notes 1. 2. 45 and 4. 2. 29.

11. *proceeders* a quibble, as Malone noted, on the academic term 'to proceed Master of Arts.'

13. *none* (Rowe) F. 'me'

15–20. Is Shakespeare capable of such verse, so trivial, so empty, and containing lines like

> For such a one as leaves a gentleman,
> And makes a god of such a cullion?

29. *to woo* F. 'ro woo' Cf. note l. 10 above.

31. *her withal* (F 3) F. 'them withall'

36. *oath,* F. 'oath.'

43. S.D. F. gives no 'exit' for Hortensio.

50–8. *I'faith...chattering tongue.* Tranio seems to know much more of Hortensio's plans than the information he has just received would warrant. Hortensio has said nothing about his widow or of calling at Petruchio's house on the way. The passage has some connexion with the alteration which has affected Hortensio's part throughout the play. Cf. pp. 124–26.

57. *eleven and twenty long* i.e. just right, v. G. 'two and thirty,' and 1. 2. 32–3.

58. S.D. F. 'Enter Biondello.'

61. *An ancient angel* v. G. 'angel.'

63. *mercatantè* (Capell) F. 'Marcantant' The F. reading is clearly a blunder, perhaps by the transcriber, for the Italian form, which indeed with its four syllables is required by the metre. On the other hand, such usages are unlike Shakespeare.

65. *countenance* F. 'eountenance'

69. *Minola,* F. 'Minola.'

71. F. gives this line the speech-heading 'Par.' v. p. 115.

Take in (Theobald) F. 'Take me'—a minim error, 'inne' taken for 'me' Cf. 2. 1. 323 (note).

S.D. F. 'Enter a Pedant.'

81–7. *'Tis death for any one* etc. Marshall points out that Tranio borrows this story from the plot of *Errors* (1. 1. 16–22).

83. *Your ships* Mantua like Padua (v. 1. 1. 2 note) is imagined to be a port.

86. *are newly* (Collier) F. 'are but newly'—a careless repetition of the 'but' earlier in the line.

95. *Pisa...citizens* A repetition of line 1. 1. 10.

106. *Vincentio—* F. 'Vincentio.'

121. *with me, sir* (F2) F. 'with me' One of the little verbal omissions which are characteristic of this text, cf. pp. 97–8.

S.D. F. 'Exeunt.'

4.3.

F. heads this scene 'Actus Quartus. Scena Prima.' v. p. 127.

S.D. F. 'Enter Katherina and Grumio.'

2. *appears*. So F. 7. *entreat*, F. 'intreat;'

9. *sleep*, F. 'ſleepe:' 10. *fed:* F. 'fed,'—transposed pointing.

13. *say*— F. 'ſay.'

14. *death*. 19. *meat*. 22. *choleric*. 32. *meat*. All periods in F.

31. S.D. F. 'Beats him'

32. *the very name* i.e. the mere name.

35. S.D. F. 'Enter Petruchio, and Hortenſio with meate.' For Hortensio's appearance here v. note 4.2.50–8 and pp. 124–26. The corresponding S.D. in *A Shrew* is worth quoting here as it may embody the stage-tradition: 'Enter Ferando with a peece of meate vppon his daggers point and Polidor with him.' It is more likely however, to have been borrowed from Marlowe, who employs the same idea in 1 *Tamburlaine*, 4.4.

43. *sorted to no proof* i.e. resulted in nothing.

60. S.D. F. 'Enter Tailor.'

61. *Come, tailor* etc. 'In our poet's time,' comments Malone, 'women's gowns were usually made by men'; and he quotes from Lyly's *Euphues and his England* (Epistle to the Ladies and Gentlewomen): 'If a Tailour make your gowne too little, you couer his fault with a broad stomacher, if too great, with a number of plights, if too short, with a faire garde, if too long, with a false gathering' (ed. Bond, ii. 10).

62. S.D. F. 'Enter Haberdaſher.'

63. *Here is the cap* etc. F. heads this line 'Fel.', v. pp. 117–18. All married women wore caps or hats both indoors and out of doors at this period, v. Sh.Eng. ii. 97.

69–72. *I'll have no bigger...not till then.* Hickson (*Notes & Queries*, Mar. 30, 1850) cites the parallel from *A Shrew* (sc. xi. 47–9):

For I will home againe vnto my fathers houſe.
Feran. I, when you'r meeke and gentell but not
Before, I know your Stomacke is not yet come downe,

and notes that Petruchio's retort is not merely misplaced but detached from its 'suggestive cue,' viz. Katharine's use of the word 'gentlewomen.' v. pp. 122–23.

71. *When you are gentle* etc. The occasions when Petruchio shows his real intentions are so rare as to be worth notice when they occur. But at the first touch of the whip the mare bolts, so he returns to his old methods in the speech following. It is her last fling, however.

76. *ears.* So F.

81. *is a paltry* (F 2) F. 'is paltrie' Cf. p. 97.

86. F. gives the haberdasher no 'exit.'

87. *masquing-stuff* v. G.

88. *like a* (F 2) F. 'like' Cf. p. 97.

97. *mar it to the time* i.e. ruin it for ever; v. G. 'time.'

98. *hop* Tailors were supposed to be hopping, skipping mortals. There is a quibble on 'hope' in l. 99. For 'kennel' v. G.

109–10. *Thou yard* etc. These references to the diminutive size of the tailor suggest that the part was played by a boy; cf. p. 119.

110. *nit* v. G. a favourite word with Nashe, found elsewhere in Shakespeare only in *L.L.L.* 4. 1. 147.

123–26. *Thou hast faced...nor braved.* The reporter's version in *A Shrew* (sc. xiii. 35–40) runs:

San. Dooſt thou heare Taylor, thou haſt braued
Many men: braue not me.
Thou'ſt faſte many men.
Taylor. Well ſir.
San. Face not me Ile nether be faſte nor braued
At thy handes I can tell thee.

Here, as Hickson noted (v. pp. 122–23), the reporter

'has carried away the words, but by transposing them and with the change of one expression—"men" for "things"—has lost the spirit: there is a pun no longer. He might have played upon "brav'd," but there he does not wait for the tailor's answer; and "fac'd," as he has it, can be understood but in one sense, and the tailor's admission becomes meaningless.'

126. *braved.* So F. 128. *pieces:* F. 'peeces.'

132. *Imprimis* F. 'Inprimis'

133–35. *Master, if ever...brown thread* This appears in *A Shrew* (sc. xiii. 28–30) as follows:

> Maiſter if euer I ſayd looſe bodies gowne,
> Sew me in a ſeame and beate me to death,
> With a bottome of browne thred.

Here the reporter is very close but the difference is enough to show his hand. '"Sew me in the skirts of it" has meaning, whereas the variation has none' (Hickson, v. note ll. 123–26 above).

133. *loose-bodied gown* Grumio's indignation gains point when we realise that, as Steevens notes, 'loose bodied gowns were the dress of harlots' in Shakespeare's day, citing Middleton, *Michaelmas Term*, 1607 (Dodsley, 1780, iii. 479) 'Dost dream of virginity now? remember a loose bodied gown, wench, and let it go.' Note that *A Shrew* here suggestively reads 'loose bodies gowne.'

149. *bill* with the stock quibble upon 'bill' = a weapon.

151–52. *he shall have no odds* We suggest that Hortensio quibblingly refers to the little pieces of cloth left over from the garment which the tailor would regard as his perquisites.

155. *Go, take it up* etc. i.e. take it away and let your master make what use he can of it. Grumio, of course, interprets it in his own fashion.

166. S.D. F. 'Exit Tail.'

167–72. *Well, come my Kate*, etc. This, which is one of the best-known passages in the play and undoubtedly Shakespearian, is thus reported in *A Shrew* (sc. xiii):

> Come Kate we now will go ſee thy fathers houſe
> Euen in theſe honeſt meane abilliments,
> Our purſes ſhallbe rich, our garments plaine,
> To ſhrowd our bodies from the winter rage
> And thats inough, what ſhould we care for more.

It is clear as Hickson notes that the reporter has Shakespeare's lines in mind, though he cheapens the whole and misses the point. Cf. note ll. 123–26 above and pp. 122–23.

170. *rich*, F. 'rich.'

172. *habit*. So F. 178. *array*. So F.

179. *account'st* (Rowe) F. 'accountedſt' Shakespeare probably wrote 'accounts'; cf. note 4. 1. 93.

194. S.D. F. gives no 'exeunt.'

4. 4.

S.D. F. 'Enter Tranio, and the Pedant dreſt like Vincentio.' For *booted* v. note l. 17 below.

1. *Sir* (Theobald) F. 'Sirs'

2. *what else?* i.e. certainly.

5. *Where we were lodgers* etc. F. prints this line as part of Tranio's speech, a mistake which Dr W. W. Greg comments upon (privately) as follows: 'Nothing is commoner in play-books than bad aligning of speakers' names, which were often supplied after the text was written. In *Believe as you List* Massinger's lining is often bad, and in one place the name is clearly a line too low. If the rules dividing the speeches were at all unclear, wrong division of the speeches was always easy.'

at the Pegasus This reference to an inn-sign reminds us again of *Errors*, e.g. 'at the Centaur' (2. 2. 2), 'at the Phœnix' (2. 2. 11). Steevens comments:

'Shakespeare has taken a sign out of London, and hung it up in Padua [Genoa]....The Pegasus is the arms of the Middle-Temple, and from that circumstance became a popular sign.'

8. S.D. F. 'Enter Biondello.'—at l. 7.

17. S.D. F. 'Enter Baptista and Lucentio: Pedant booted and bare headed.'—after l. 18. As the Pedant has already been on the stage for 17 lines and is carefully described on entry as 'dreſt like Vincentio' the F. 'booted' comes in here in strangely belated fashion, and even 'bare headed,' though no doubt polite to Baptista, is an unusual way of expressing 'puts off his hat.' It seems probable, in short, that the scene originally opened with this S.D. and the dialogue that follows; and that, when the previous 17 lines were added in revision, the S.D. was left as it was except for the deletion of Tranio's name. The fact that F. repeats the speech-heading 'Tra.' at the beginning of l. 19 lends support to this theory. For a similar phenomenon v. note 4. 1. 170 S.D.

23, 24. F. prints these as one line.

30. *to him,* F. 'to him:'

32. *matched:* F. 'matcht,'

54. *happily* i.e. haply, v. G.

58. *your servant here* i.e. Lucentio who as Cambio the schoolmaster had become Baptista's 'servant,' as Florio, for instance, was 'servant' to the Earl of Southampton. Failing to appreciate this or the stage-business that takes place a few lines below, Clark and Wright proposed to read 'Biondello' for 'Cambio' at l. 62.

S.D. *he winks* etc. Cf. l. 74 below.

59. *My boy* Biondello, of course.

61. *pittance* i.e. scanty meal, v. G.

62–3. F. divides 'It likes me well:/Cambio...readie ſtraight:'

67. *I pray* etc. Rowe and many others give this speech to Lucentio, v. next note.

68. *get thee gone* i.e. to 'fetch the scrivener' (v. l. 59) and to call at St Luke's church on the way (l. 99). There is no difficulty here as many edd. seem to imagine (v. P. A. Daniel, *Time-Analysis*, p. 167).

S.D. F. 'Exit.'—after l. 67. After l. 68 F. reads 'Enter Peter' a S.D. received in silent despair by all edd. except Bond, who suggests that this Peter is 'some servant come to warn Tranio that his meal is ready.' This seems to us a perfectly satisfactory explanation, if as we suppose 'Peter' is the name of an actor (v. p. 118). It is clear also that Tranio-Lucentio's lodging and Baptista's house both open upon the stage in this scene, though apparently only the sharp-eyed P. A. Daniel has noticed it.

72. 'Exeunt.'/'Enter Lucentio and Biondello.' This second S.D. is quite unnecessary, since the two have only stood aside. We suspect adaptation here, on other grounds, chiefly that Biondello's off-hand, not to say impertinent, manner with Lucentio-Cambio in the dialogue which follows suggests that the writer of the dialogue has forgotten Cambio's real identity. The boy calls him Cambio throughout, it will be noticed.

89–90. *cum privilegio* etc. The inscription often found on title-pages of books at this period. Strictly and originally it means 'with the privilege for printing only' (v. A. W. Reed, *Early Tudor Drama*, pp. 176–86), but later it came to be understood 'with the privilege of sole printing,' as Biondello certainly understands it here. It may be noted that Biondello is surprisingly bookish in this dialogue; cf. 'appendix' in l. 101.

imprimendum solum (F 2) F. 'Impremendum ſolem'

90. *church!* (Bond) F. 'Church' Most edd. read 'church;'

101. *appendix* Biondello means attendant, one that follows behind. The jest is also found in Nashe's *Unfortunate Traveller*, 1594 (McKerrow, ii. 209) 'a certain kind of appendix or page' (i.e. page-boy).

S.D. F. 'Exit.'

103. *doubt* Pope read 'doubt her' to rhyme with the two following lines.

105. S.D. F. 'Exit.'

4. 5.

S.D. F. 'Enter Petruchio, Kate, Hortentio' The fact that the party is obviously walking and that the horses have gone on before fixes the scene as a hill along the highway.

18. *Then* F. 'theu' *blessed, it is* (F 2) F. 'bleſt, it in'

25. *unluckily against the bias* v. G. 'bias.' The bowl should run according to the bias unless it is turned aside by accident.

26. *what company* (Steevens) F. 'Company'

S.D. F. 'Enter Vincentio.'

30. *Such war of white and red* etc. Bond quotes *V.A.* 345–46:

> To note the fighting conflict of her hue,
> How white and red each other did destroy,

and supposes that 'the poet of *Henry VI* and *Richard III*' is glancing at the Wars of the Roses.

31–2. *What stars...face?* Bond, quoting Craig, compares *Son.* 132:

> Nor that full star that ushers in the even
> Doth half that glory to the sober west
> As those two mourning eyes become thy face.

35–6. *a woman* (F 2) F. 'the woman'

38. *Whither...where* (F 2) F. 'Whether...whether' Probably a case of incorrect expansion by the compositor, 'where' being a contracted form of 'whether.' For instance 'where' in l. 27 above may, as Capell suggested, stand for 'whither.'

41. *Allot* (Pope) F. 'A lots'

63. *Thy son by this hath married* As P. A. Daniel (*Time-Analysis*, p. 168) points out, this is a piece of knowledge Petruchio could not possibly possess; still

less could Hortensio, who confirms it at l. 74, since both he and Tranio (whom of course Petruchio and he take to be Lucentio) had forsworn Bianca in 4. 2. A message from Padua to Petruchio before leaving home would have put all right, and perhaps such a message was 'cut' in the process of revision. An audience, however, would not be likely to perceive anything amiss.

76. S.D. F. 'Exeunt.' Bond, who reads 'Exeunt all but Hortensio' with most mod. edd., comments: 'Their roads part, Hortensio's widow being imagined as Petruchio's neighbour.' On the contrary, 5. 2. 13–6 shows that the widow lived in Padua. All that happens here is that as the party moves off Hortensio is left last upon the stage.

78. *she be froward* (F 2) F. 'ſhe froward' Cf. pp. 97–8.

79. S.D. F. 'Exit.'

5. 1.

S.D. F. 'Enter Biondello, Lucentio and Bianea, Gremio is out before.' The text gives us no clue why Gremio is thus 'out before,' except to tell us (l. 8) that he is waiting for Cambio, whom of course he regards as his secret go-between with Bianca. There is some kind of dramatic loose-end here. The promising relations between Gremio and Lucentio have stood still since 1. 2. 138–56, and one can imagine that the plot might have received a pretty additional complication had Bianca, assuring Gremio as well she might that she would never marry Tranio-Lucentio, led him to suppose that Lucentio-Cambio would assist her to elope with him. If so, he would be naturally enough waiting outside Baptista's house at this juncture. It is even conceivable that he had a hand in engaging the old priest at St Luke's.

The S D. 'Gremio is out before' is interesting, if not

unique, from the theatrical point of view; but we do not observe that the authorities on the Elizabethan Stage have commented upon it.

4. S.D. F. 'Exit.'

6. *o'your back* The meaning is doubtful: either 'at your back' i.e. I'll see you leave the church, or 'on your back' i.e. I'll see you into church. *master's* (Capell) F. 'miſtris' Cf. notes l. 51 (below) and 1. 2. 18.

8. S.D. F. 'Enter Petruchio, Kate, Vincentio, Grumio with Attendants.'

9–10. *Sir, here's the door...market-place* These lines, if nothing else, justify our setting of 'the square in Padua' with Baptista's house and Tranio's lodging opening upon it. Cf. 1. 1. head-note.

12. *go;* F. 'go,' 13. *here,* F. 'here;'—transposed pointing.

14. S.D. F. 'Knock.'

16. S.D. F. 'Pedant lookes out of the window.' 'The window' means of course the stage-window. Most edd. have assumed it to be the window at the back of the upper-stage. It seems far more likely to have been one of the windows above the side-doors, i.e. that above the door into 'Lucentio's house,' v. note 1. 1. 252 S.D.

30. *from Mantua* (Malone) F. 'from Padua' Clark and Wright attempt to justify the F. reading thus: 'The Pedant has been staying some time at Padua, and that is all he means.' Surely this is far-fetched. A much better jest is that the Pedant should name the place from which he had himself come, forgetting, Malone notes, 'as might well happen, that the real Vincentio was of Pisa.' Shakespearian texts, moreover, are prone to confuse the names of these Italian cities (cf. *Two Gent.* 2. 5. 1; 3. 1. 81; 5. 4. 130).

31. *and is here* (Dyce) F. 'and here' Cf. pp. 97–8.

39. S.D. F. 'Enter Biondello.'

42. *brought* F. 'brough'

44. *crack-hemp* v. G. A possible link with Gascoigne's *Supposes* which gives us 'cracke-halter' at 1. 4. 6. Cf. pp. xiv, xviii–xix.

45. *I hope I may choose, sir* i.e. allow me, sir!—spoken to a disagreeable person who bars one's path in the street; v. G. 'choose.'

51. *master's* (F 2) F. 'Miſtris' Cf. notes l. 6 above and 1. 2. 18.

54. S.D. F. 'He beates Biondello.'

56. S.D. F. gives no 'exit,' but it is clear that Biondello goes out at this point to tell Lucentio and Bianca what has happened.

57. S.D. F. again gives no 'exit.'

59. S.D. F. 'Enter Pedant with ſeruants, Baptiſta, Tranio.'

72. *'cerns* This contracted form in prose arouses suspicion, and true enough if we look close we find that it forms part of a fossil line of verse—

What 'cerns it you, if I wear pearl and gold?

80. *Tranio* F. 'Tronio'

103–104. The original verse begins to break through the reviser's prose here.

105. S.D. F. 'Enter Biondello, Lucentio and Biancu.'—after l. 104.

106. *and—yonder* (Capell) F. 'and yonder'

108. S.D. F. 'Kneele.' and after l. 107 'Exit Biondello, Tranio and Pedant as faſt as may be.' Cf. p. 100.

113. *counterfeit supposes* An obvious link with Gascoigne's play. Cf. note l. 44 above.

114–15. *Here's packing...us all* This seems to suggest that Gremio has been hoodwinked also.

120. *miracles.* So F.

123. *at last* (F 2) F. 'at the laſt' Cf. pp. 97–8.

132. S.D. F. 'Exit.'

133. S.D. F. 'Exit.'

134. S.D. F. 'Exeunt.'

135. *My cake is dough* Cf. 1. 1. 109 and v. G. 'dough.'

dough, but F. 'doug, hbut'

136. S.D. F. gives no 'exit.'

141. *No* F. 'Mo' 144. *Kate*. So F.

145. S.D. F. 'Exeunt.'

5. 2.

F. heads this scene 'Actus Quintus.'

S.D. F. 'Enter Baptiſta, Vincentio, Gremio, the Pedant, Lucentio, and Bianca. Tranio, Biondello Grumio, and Widdow: The Seruingmen with Tranio bringing in a Banquet.' The repetition of 'Tranio' suggests that the last part of the S.D. was a later addition. Note the remarkable omission of Hortensio, Petruchio and Katharina—the travellers; were they intended in some earlier draft to enter unexpectedly upon the scene? For 'banquet' v. G.

2. *done* (Rowe) F. 'come' Cf. p. 103.

4–5. *bid my father welcome* etc. From this it is clear that Lucentio had bidden the whole party to a 'banquet' at his house after the 'great good cheer' of the bridal feast at Baptista's.

7. *widow,* F. 'Widdow:' F. prints 'Widdow' in italics as if it were a proper name.

11. S.D. Capell read here 'Company sit to Table.' The table is doubtful, however, at an after-dinner banquet, and Lucentio's 'For now we sit to chat, as well as eat' suggests easy chairs about the room.

16. *fears* The word might mean both 'frightens' and 'is afraid of.' Hence the widow's misapprehension.

22. *Thus I conceive by him* i.e. That's what I take him for.

32. *I am mean, indeed, respecting you.* i.e. I am mild compared with you. Kyd twice (*Span. Trag.* 3. 1. 98; *Sol. & Pers.* 1. 5. 39) uses the word in this sense.

35. *put her down* Steevens quotes *Ado*, 2. 1. 263–66.

37. *ha' to thee* (F 2) F. 'ha to the'

S.D. F. 'Drinkes to Hortentio.'

39. *butt* F. 'But' Rowe and many edd. read 'butt heads' so as to give point to Bianca's retort. Possibly the line should run 'Believe me, they butt heads together well.'

44. *shall not:* F. 'ſhall not' *begun,* F. 'begun:' Capell first rectified the pointing.

45. *bitter* (Theobald) F. 'better' *two* (F 3) F. 'too' Cf. l. 62 and p. 103.

46–7. *Am I your bird* etc. Bianca refers to the fowling methods of the time. Birds were only shot sitting in a bush or tree; if therefore the bird shifted its bush, the fowler had to follow.

48. *You are welcome all* Apparently the customary words of the hostess when making the move to leave the men to their wine and talk.

S.D. F. 'Exit Bianca.' But it is clear that the other women go with her.

49. *Signior Tranio* This title sits oddly upon the son of a 'sail-maker in Bergamo' (5. 1. 74).

62. *two* (Rowe) F. 'too'

65. *therefore for* (F 2) F. 'therefore ſir'

70. *What is* (Steevens) F. 'What's'

77. S.D. F. 'Exit.' 78. *I will* (Capell) F. 'Ile'

79. S.D. F. 'Enter Biondello.'

82–3. *How! she is...an answer?* F. prints this as prose.

82. *she is* (Capell) F. 'ſhe's'

85. *I hope better.* i.e. I entertain better hopes. By placing a comma after 'hope' edd. have made 'better' refer to 'answer,' and thus given a hesitating note to Petruchio's calm assurance.

86–90. *Sirrah Biondello* etc. F. prints as prose.

87. S.D. F. 'Exit. Bion.'

89. S.D. F. 'Enter Biondello.'

93–4. F. divides 'Worſe...come:/Oh vilde... indur'd:'

96. S.D. F. 'Exit.'

98. S.D. F. 'Enter Katerina.'

102. *parlour* F. 'Parler'

105. S.D. F. gives no 'exit.'

106. *of wonder* (S. Walker) F. 'of a wonder' Cf. pp. 97–8.

109. *awful* i.e. commanding respect (not 'terrible').

supremacy F. 'ſupremicie'

118. *obedience* The word has been caught by the compositor's eye from the previous line and substituted for another. There are various guesses, e.g. 'her gentleness,' 'her patience,' 'submission.'

S.D. F. 'Enter Kate, Bianca, and Widdow.'

128. *cost one hundred* (Singer) F. 'coſt me fiue hundred'—which is typical of the petty carelessness of this text throughout. The reading usually accepted is Rowe's 'cost me an hundred.' But if we take the F. 'me' to be a misprint or mistranscription of 'one' (cf. note 1. 2. 170), we get good sense, good metre, and an explanation of the F. error, the 'fiue' in that case being a makeshift emendation of the players.

130–32. *Katharine, I charge thee* etc. F. prints as prose.

132. *you're* F. 'your' This is unusual for Shakespeare who generally writes 'yar' or 'yare.'

136–79. This famous speech, though very different in content, is strikingly similar both in build and rhythm to Berowne's equally famous speech in *L.L.L.* (4. 3. 286 et seq.).

136. *threatening* F. 'thretaning'

138. *governor:* F. 'Gouernour.'

148. *maintenance commits* (Clark & Wright) F. 'maintenance. Commits' Shakespeare's fondness for an initial capital C (v. Sh.Hand, pp. 115–16) seems to have led astray transcriber, compositor, and all edd. down to 1863.

173. *straws*, F. 'ſtrawes:'

176–79. *Then vail...do him ease.* Hickson (v. pp. 122–23) quotes the parallel passage from *A Shrew* (sc. xviii):

> Laying our handes vnder theire feete to tread,
> If that by that we might procure there eaſe,
> And for a preſident Ile firſt begin,
> And lay my hand vnder my huſbands feete,

and notes that, though 'the imitator, as usual, has caught something of the words of the original, which he has laboured to reproduce at a most unusual sacrifice of grammar and sense,' he has by omitting the words 'in token of which duty' omitted the whole point of the passage.

176. *vail your stomachs* i.e. lower your pride.

it is no boot i.e. there is no help for it.

177. *place your hands...foot* There is clearly some reference here to a traditional act of some kind expressing allegiance or servitude.

184–85. *Come Kate...are sped* The corresponding lines in *A Shrew* (sc. xviii) are:

> Tis Kate and I am wed, and you are ſped.
> And ſo farwell for we will to our beds.

'Is it not evident,' comments Hickson (v. pp. 122–23) 'that Shakespeare chose the word "sped" as a rhyme to "bed," and that the imitator, in endeavouring to recollect the jingle, has not only spoiled the rhyme but missed the fact that "three" were "married," notwithstanding that "two" were "sped"?'

186. *white* v. G. As Dr Johnson notes, there is a quibble in the name Bianca.

187. *And, being a winner*, etc. 'alluding to the natural wish of successful gamesters to leave the table before their luck turns' (Bond).

S.D. F. 'Exit Petruchio.'

188. *shrow* So F., the usual spelling.

189. S.D. F. gives no 'Exeunt.'

THE STAGE-HISTORY OF
THE TAMING OF THE SHREW

Henslowe's note that 'the tamynge of A Shrowe' was one of the plays acted at Newington Butts in June, 1594, when the Admiral's and the Chamberlain's companies were there, is discussed elsewhere in this volume (pp. xiii, xxiii, 106). Sir E. K. Chambers (*Elizabethan Stage*, ii. 197) and others are inclined to think that *Loue Labours Wonne*, mentioned by Meres in *Palladis Tamia* (1598), is *The Taming of the Shrew*. Sir Henry Herbert, Master of the Revels, recorded that *The Taminge of the Shrew* was acted at St James's before the King and Queen on November 26, 1633, and 'likt'; and the performance of a 'Revived Play Taminge the Shrew' is mentioned in his rough accounts for 1663–64 (J. Q. Adams, *Dramatic Records of Sir Henry Herbert*, pp. 53 and 138). In the division of December, 1660, the play had fallen to Killigrew; and on April 9, 1667, Pepys saw at the King's house 'The Tameing of a Shrew, which hath some very good pieces in it, but generally is but a mean play; and the best part, Sawny, done by Lacy, hath not half its life, by reason of the words, I suppose, not being understood, at least by me.' On November 1, 1667, he again saw the play at the King's house, 'a silly play and an old one.' Though he calls it 'The Taming of a Shrew,' it was, in fact, *Sauny the Scott: or, The Taming of the Shrew*, an adaptation of Shakespeare's play by John Lacy, of the King's company. By the time it found its way into print, in 1698, Sauny was being played by Bullock, Petruchio by Powell, Margaret (the Shrew) by Mrs Verbruggen and Bianca by Mrs Cibber; but Lacy was the first and the great Sauny. The name came from Sander, the character in the 1594 *Taming of a Shrew* which corresponds to Grumio, and the original Sander and principal player in the Induction was possibly the Elizabethan actor, Alexander Cooke (cf. pp. 119–20). It may have been the name which gave Lacy the hint for turning him into a Scot and writing his part in a language at which Pepys is not the only hearer or reader to have boggled. Lacy wrote his play in prose, cut out the Induction and the little interlude, and, by way of improving the fun, wrote up the part of Sauny, introduced a bedroom scene in which Sauny is to undress Margaret (there being no women in the house), and made Petruchio force the shrew to smoke a pipe, vow she has toothache and send for a barber to draw the tooth, and vow she is dead and send for a bier and a funeral procession. His play was very popular; and upon it, much more than on Shakespeare's, was founded the ballad-farce of two acts (published in or about 1735), *A Cure for a Scold*, written by J. Worsdale, who calls himself 'portrait-painter' on his title-page, and acted at Drury Lane in February, 1735, with Macklin as Manly (Petruchio), Mrs Clive as Peg (Katharine), Mrs Pritchard as Flora, her sister, and Salway as Archer, an anglicized, refined and diminished Sauny. Worsdale retained the tooth-drawing, but not the undressing nor the bier; he altered the Bianca plot considerably and put in many songs of his own writing.

Another plan was followed by Charles Johnson in his *Cobler of Preston*, produced at Drury Lane on February 3, 1716, with Pinkethman as Kit Sly, Ryan as Sir Charles Briton (the Lord), Mrs Willis as Sly's wife and Mrs Baker as Cicely Gundy, an ale-wife; and also by Christopher Bullock, of the rival company, in his farce with the same title, which was produced at Lincoln's Inn Fields on January 24, 1716, with Ogden as Sir Jasper Manly (the Lord), Spiller as Toby Guzzle (Sly), the author and his son as Snuffle, a Puritan, and Grist, a miller, and Hall and Griffin in the female parts of Dame Hacket, an ale-wife, and

Dorcas, the wife of Guzzle. Both farces were published in 1716; and Bullock in his preface boasts of having written his play in two days and got it staged in three, because he knew that Johnson's was in rehearsal at Drury Lane. He must have known something more about Johnson's farce than that, because both plays take the Induction only and elaborate it. Of the two, Bullock's is the livelier. Guzzle, made as part of the jest to act as a magistrate, sends his squabbling wife and Dame Hacket to be ducked; and in judging the Puritan and the miller, who have been making free with each other's wives, lectures Snuffle with sudden and allusive eloquence. Johnson, with the events of the '15 in his mind, drags in a good deal of politics; and, writing partly in prose and partly in verse, makes it part of the jest that Sly shall be persuaded he is a Spaniard in Spain and threatened with death for high treason. Politics and Pinkethman won some success for Johnson's dull play; but when it was turned into a musical farce in two acts, *The Cobbler of Preston* (published in 1817), and played at Drury Lane in September, 1817, the politics were cut out, a love-story was put in, and Munden was exceedingly droll as Sly.

Sauny the Scot went on being acted at Drury Lane, Lincoln's Inn Fields and the Queen's, and also at Goodman's Fields, until it was replaced by Garrick's *Catharine and Petruchio.* The first definite mention of this play records its performance at Drury Lane on January 21, 1756; but it seems probable that it was first seen at the same theatre on March 18, 1754, when Mrs Pritchard, at her benefit, acted Catharine in a piece of this title. In 1756 and later the Catharine was Mrs Clive. Woodward, as Petruchio, was reported to have paid off old scores by handling her very roughly, and Mrs Clive to have retaliated by almost convincing the audience that 'Petruchio was not so lordly as he assumed to be.' The Grumio was Yates. Garrick left out the Induction: but his condensation (three acts, in verse, apparently not published till 1780) of the comedy, acted by the travelling players, was an adroit piece of work, in spite of a few absurdities inevitable in condensation. It preserved far more of Shakespeare than Lacy or Worsdale had, and omitted the worst of their additions. It became so popular as an after-piece that it held the stage till the second half of the nineteenth century, and was revived, as a curiosity, by Beerbohm Tree at Her Majesty's Theatre in November, 1897. Shuter, King, Dodd, Lewis and Palmer all played Petruchio; among the Catharines were Mrs Hamilton, Mrs Green, Mrs Abington, Miss Pope, Mrs Wrighten and Miss Sorace; and Shuter, Baddeley and Quick were seen as Grumio. Kemble liked playing Petruchio. Once or twice, in 1788 and 1789, Mrs Siddons obliged him by acting Katharine (as he spelled the name), and Mrs Charles Kemble was good in the part. Macready also kept to Garrick's version, which, like Kemble, he slightly altered; and it was *Catharine and Petruchio* which the ineluctable Frederic Reynolds turned into an opera (too late for mention in his autobiography), with an overture by Rossini, and songs taken from here, there and everywhere in Shakespeare's works and set to music composed and selected by Braham and T. Cooke. When the opera was first staged, at Drury Lane, in May, 1828, with fine scenery by Stanfield and others, Miss Ayton was the Catharine, Wallack the Petruchio, Harley the Grumio and Braham the Hortensio.

Shakespeare's *The Taming of the Shrew* had to wait longer than any other of his plays for restoration to the stage. The restoration, when it came, took a surprising form. In 1837 Benjamin Webster began his admirable management of the Haymarket Theatre. In March, 1844, to celebrate the return to the stage of Mrs Nisbett (then Lady Boothby), he commissioned J. R. Planché to prepare a revival of the play as Shakespeare wrote it, Induction and all. Planché anticipated the ideas of Mr William Poel by staging the play in what he meant to be the Elizabethan manner. In this revival, the Hortensio was Howe, whom many can still remember as a veteran actor in Henry Irving's company at the Lyceum; and to Irving's friend and fellow-worker, Frank Marshall, Howe described the staging thus: 'The Lord and his servants were seated on the left-hand corner of the stage in the first entrance: Sly and his party on the right hand. A large drapery of maroon-coloured curtains looped up, with inner curtains of tapestry, stretched completely across the stage; there was a division in the centre of the latter through which the various characters made their exits and entrances. At the beginning of each scene, one of the troupe of actors removed the old placard, and hung a fresh one denoting the place in which the action was to be represented.' The characters of the Induction were kept on the stage the whole time, and at the end Sly was carried off, dead drunk, in dumb show. In the performance of 1844 Mrs Nisbett played Katharine; Webster, Petrucio (as he first chose to spell it); Strickland, Sly; Mrs Seymour, Bianca; and Buckstone, Grumio. The cast was changed for a revival in 1847, when Lambert acted Sly and Keeley, Grumio. Webster was, not unduly, proud of this achievement, and tried to intensify its Elizabethan flavour by making-up players in the Induction to look like Shakespeare, Ben Jonson and Tarleton, and by showing a drop-scene with a view of Elizabethan London, including the Globe playhouse.

Though *Catharine and Petruchio* was not ousted, *The Taming of the Shrew* had come back. Samuel Phelps staged it at Sadler's Wells in 1856, taking the part of Sly. But the play did not become popular until Augustin Daly gave it a new impetus. In New York *Catharine and Petruchio* had held the stage with success ever since Hallam, an excellent Petruchio, with Margaret Cheer as Catharine, had produced it at the John-street Theatre in 1768. Hodgkinson and Harper had also been successful as Petruchio, and Mrs Seymour,

Miss Westray and Mrs Johnson as Catharine; and in 1800 Jefferson had appeared as Grumio. The Douglass company had acted Garrick's piece in Philadelphia, and others elsewhere. Shakespeare's play was staged for the first time in America at Daly's Theatre, New York, on January 18, 1887, with Ada Rehan as Katharine and John Drew as Petruchio. On May 29, 1888, the same production was shown at the Gaiety Theatre in London; and in spite of Daly's unnecessary alterations in the order of scenes (with which London then first became acquainted) the acting and the staging won it instant favour. The play was chosen for the opening performance at the new Daly's Theatre in London on March 12, 1893; and Ada Rehan's Katharine remains in the memory of playgoers as a work of genius.

Since then the play has been much acted. Lacking the Induction, it was in the repertory of the Benson company, which performed it often in London and at Stratford-upon-Avon. Mr Oscar Asche produced it first at the Adelphi Theatre in November, 1904, and he has been not infrequently seen since as Sly and Petruchio, with Miss Lily Brayton as Katharine. On May 12, 1913, Sir John Martin-Harvey first showed London, at the Prince of Wales's Theatre, his production of the play in the Elizabethan manner. The Oxford University Dramatic Society gave it at Oxford in February, 1907; the Birmingham Repertory Theatre in June, 1918. The 'Old Vic.' company chose it for their opening performance at the Lyric Theatre, Hammersmith, in September, 1927; and in the same month it was produced in the Elizabethan manner at the Maddermarket Theatre, Norwich. In Germany the comedy seems to have been known at least as early as 1705, when Christian Weise's *Comedy of the angry Catharine* was performed; and Petruchio is one of the parts in the repertory of Albert Bassermann.

[1928] HAROLD CHILD.

GLOSSARY

Note. Where a pun or quibble is intended, the meanings are distinguished as (*a*) and (*b*)

ACCORD, concord, harmony; 3. 1. 73

ÆACIDES, the descendants of ÆACUS—for example Ajax, the son of Telamon, the son of Æacus, the son of Jupiter; 3. 1. 52

AFFY, betroth; 4. 4. 49

AGENOR, the father of Europa, who was carried off by Jupiter in the form of a bull; 1. 1. 167

AGLET-BABY, a small figure forming the tag of a point or lace (from the Fr. 'aiguillette'); 1. 2. 78

ALL-AMORT, sick to death, dejected (from the Fr. 'à la mort'); 4. 3. 36

ALLA NOSTRA CASA BEN VENUTO, welcome to our house; 1. 2. 25

ANGEL, a gold coin worth 10*s*.; 'an ancient angel' = a fellow of the good old stamp, as distinguished from the debased coinage of the day—a common jest, cf. Cotgrave (1611) '*Angelot*...an old angel, and by metaphor, a fellow of th'old, sound, honest and worthie stamp'; 4. 2. 61

ANTIC, buffoon, fantastic; Ind. i. 100

APPENDIX, jocularly used for 'one who follows behind,' i.e. a page; 4. 4. 101

ARGOSY, 'a merchant vessel of the largest size and burden, esp. those of Ragusa and Venice' N.E.D. (cf. *M.V.* 1. 1. 9); 2. 1. 367, 369

ARRAS COUNTERPOINTS, v. *counterpoints*; 2. 1. 344

ASKANCE, scornful; lit. 'to look askance' = to look sideways, askew—an action which might imply scorn, envy, or (in the only mod. sense) suspicion; 2. 1. 241

AWFUL, commanding respect; 5. 2. 109

BACKARE! stand back! The origin of the expression is obscure; 2. 1. 73

BALK LOGIC, chop logic (N.E.D. quotes *Faerie Queene*, 3. 2. 12 'Her list in stryfull termes with him to balke'); 1. 1. 34

BALM, anoint with fragrant liquid; Ind. i. 47

BANQUET, an elaborate kind of dessert, consisting of fruit, wine, sweetmeats, etc., served at some interval after supper (cf. *Ado*, 2. 1. 158; *Rom.* 1. 5. 124; *Tim.* 1. 2. 160); 5. 2. 9

BAR IN LAW, a plea which effectually prevents an action or claim; 1. 1. 134

BASTA, enough; 1. 1. 197

BATE, flutter the wings impatiently; 4. 1. 186

BEAR-HERD, one who leads a bear about the country for exhibition; Ind. ii. 20

BEAT, flap the wings; 4. 1. 186

BEETLE, a heavy hammer or mallet; 4. 1. 148

BE-METE, measure; 4. 3. 113

BEMOIL, befoul; 4. 1. 69

BEN VENUTO, welcome; 1. 2. 278

BESTRAUGHT, distracted, out of one's mind (not a blunder-word); Ind. ii. 25

BIAS, the lead to one side of the bowl which makes it turn in that direction; 'against the bias' = against the grain; 4. 5. 25

BOARD, accost, pay address to; 1. 2. 94

BONNY, fine, big, strapping (cf. *A.Y.L.* 2. 3. 8 'the bonny prizer'); 2. 1. 186

BOOKS (in your), in your good books (v. note and cf. *Ado*, 1. 1. 74); 2. 1. 222

BOOT-HOSE, 'an over-stocking which covers the leg like a jack-boot' (N.E.D. 'boot-stocking'); 3. 2. 65

BOTS, a horse-disease caused by worms; 3. 2. 54

BOTTOM, the core of the skein upon which the thread was wound; 4. 3. 135

BOY, a term of abuse or contempt, meaning 'coward, traitor, wretch' (cf. *Cor.* 5. 6. 101–17). In early use the word is associated with 'boie' = executioner, and this throws light upon 'hangman boys' (*Two Gent.* 4. 4. 53) and Cupid as 'hangman' (*Ado*, 3. 2. 11); Ind. i. 13

BRACH, bitch; Ind. i. 17

BREATHED, in good wind; Ind. ii. 48

BREECHING SCHOLAR, schoolboy liable to be whipped (cf. Marlowe, *Ed. II*, 5. 4. 55 'Whose looks were as a breeching to a boy'); 3. 1. 18

BROACH, let blood, lit. 'tap' (cf. N.E.D. 'broach' vb[1] 4 *c*); Ind. i. 16

BUG, bogey; 1. 2. 208

BURST, smash; Ind. i. 7

BURTHEN, accompaniment, refrain (v. note); 1. 2. 67

BUTT, bottom; 'head and butt' = head and tail; 5. 2. 40, 41

BUZZ, (*a*) the buzz of a bee, (*b*) rumour, scandal; 2. 1. 206

BUZZARD, (*a*) an inferior kind of hawk, a type of stupidity because unteachable by the falconer, (*b*) moth, cockchafer; 2. 1. 206, 207, 208

CANDLE-CASE, receptacle for candle-ends; 3. 2. 45

CARD-MAKER, a 'card' was an instrument with iron teeth for combing out the fibres of wool by hand; Ind. ii. 19

CARD OF TEN, a card with ten pips, i.e. 'the highest card in the old simple games of our ancestors' (Warburton); 2. 1. 398

CART, to carry through the streets as a public exposure—the treatment of criminals, bawds and harlots (cf. 'stale' l. 58); 1. 1. 55

CATE, dainty, delicacy; 2. 1. 189

CENSER, generally explained as a perforated fumigator, but the meaning is uncertain (cf. 2 *Hen. IV*, 5. 4. 21); 4. 3. 91

CHAFE, (*a*) irritate, vex, (*b*) inflame, excite, heat; 2. 1. 235

CHAPELESS, without the chape, i.e. the metal plate on the scabbard covering the point of the sword; 3. 2. 47

CHOOSE, take one's way, be allowed to proceed (v. note and cf. *M.V.* 1. 2. 45); 5. 1. 45

CLAP UP, fix up hastily, concoct hurriedly (cf. *King John*, 3. 1. 235); 2. 1. 318

COCK'S PASSION, corruption of 'God's Passion'; 4. 1. 108

COMPASSED, cut so as to fall in a circle (cf. 'compassed window' *Troil.* 1. 2. 120); 4. 3. 137

CONCEIVE, understand the situation; 1. 2. 267

CONDITIONS, qualities, characteristics; 5. 2. 167

CONSTER, old form of 'construe'; 3. 1. 30

CONTRIVE, spend or pass the time. Very rare use, found in *Faerie Queene*, 2. 9. 48, but not elsewhere in Shakespeare; 1. 2. 272

CON TUTTO IL CUORE BEN TROVATO, with all my heart well met; 1. 2. 24

CONY-CATCH, cheat, deceive, evade; 4. 1. 40; 5. 1. 96

COPATAIN HAT, sugar-loaf hat; 5. 1. 64

COUNTERPOINTS, counterpanes (of Arras tapestry); 2. 1. 344

CRAB, (*a*) crab-apple, (*b*) cross-grained or ill-tempered person; 2. 1. 227, 228

CRACK, to make an explosive sound (cf. *Macb.* 4. 1. 117 'the crack of doom'); 1. 2. 95

CRACK-HEMP, gallows-bird; 5. 1. 44

CRAVEN, a cock that 'cried creak' or acknowledged defeat; 2. 1. 225

CRUPPER, the leather strap which passes in a loop from the saddle round the horse's tail to keep the saddle from slipping; 3. 2. 59; 4. 1. 74

CULLION, base fellow (lit. testicle); 4. 2. 20

CUM PRIVILEGIO AD IMPRIMENDUM SOLUM, with the privilege of sole printing. An inscription commonly found on contemporary title-pages to denote that the printer had a special licence to print certain kinds of book (v. note); 4. 4. 89–90

CURIOUS, particular, difficult in business matters; 4. 4. 36

CURST, shrewish; 1. 1. 179 *et passim*

CUSTARD-COFFIN, custard-pie; 4. 3. 82

DANCE BAREFOOT. The elder unmarried sister was supposed to dance barefoot at the wedding of a younger; thus the phrase became proverbial for 'to remain unmarried'; 2. 1. 33

DEMI-CANNON, a large gun with a 6½ inch bore; 4. 3. 88

DENIER, a very small French coin (= 1/12 of a sou); Ind. i. 8

DENY, refuse; 2. 1. 179; 5. 2. 103

DIGRESS, deviate; 3. 2. 105

DOMINEER, swagger, feast uproariously (cf. Nashe 'dominere in Tauernes' McKerrow, i. 166. 10); 3. 2. 222

DOUGH, 'my cake is dough,' prov. = I have failed; 1. 1. 109; 5. 1. 135

DUTY, due, reward; 4. 1. 34

ELEVEN AND TWENTY LONG, i.e. just the right length (cf. *two and thirty*); 4. 2. 57

EMBOSSED, foaming at the mouth with exhaustion, played out, dead beat; Ind. i. 16

ENTRANCE, entrance-fee; 2. 1. 54

ENVY, hate; 2. 1. 18

FACE, (*a*) trim with braid or other material, (*b*) bully; 4. 3. 123–26

FACE IT WITH A CARD OF TEN, put a bold face upon it—an expression from card-play (v. *card of ten*); 2. 1. 398

FAIR, fine; 2. 1. 17

FAIRLY, finely; 1. 2. 143

FASHIONS, i.e. 'the farcy (of our ignorant smiths called the Fashions)' G. Markham, *Masterpiece*, 1610. The farcy, or farcin, was a horse-disease closely resembling the glanders (q.v.); 3. 2. 51

FAULT, a break in the scent (v. note); Ind. i. 19

FEAR, (i) frighten, (ii) be afraid of; 1. 2. 208; 5. 2. 16–19

FEEZE, lit. 'to drive away' or 'frighten off,' and thence 'to flog.' A pot-house term often used as equivalent to the mod. phrase 'settle the hash of (a person).' Cf. *Troil.* 2. 3. 215, and *M.W.W.* 1. 3. 10 where the Host calls Falstaff his Pheazar (= Vizier), in quibbling reference to 'feeze'; Ind. i. 1

FIVES, the vives or avives, 'a swelling of the parotid glands in horses; the strangles' (N.E.D.); 3. 2. 53

FLORENTIUS, Sir Florent (a character in bk. i. of Gower's *Confessio Amantis*); 1. 2. 68

FORMAL, punctilious, ceremonious; 3. 1. 61

FRET, (*a*) of merchandise—to deteriorate through rust, moth, decay, etc., (*b*) the modern sense; 2. 1. 321

FRETS, rings of gut or bars of wood upon the lute to regulate the fingering; 2. 1. 149, 152

FURNITURE, outfit; 4. 3. 178

FUSTIAN, a coarse cloth made of cotton and flax; 4. 1. 44

GALLIASS, 'a heavy low-built vessel larger than a galley' (N.E.D.); 2. 1. 371

GAMESTER, gambler, adventurer; 2. 1. 393

GAMUT, (i) the musical scale, (ii) the name of the lowest note of the gamut. The word is a combination of *gamma*, the alphabet name, and *ut* (now *do*), the musical name; 3. 1. 67–73, 79

GLANDERS, 'a contagious disease in horses, the chief symptoms of which are swellings beneath the jaw and discharge of mucous matter from the nostrils' (N.E.D.); 3. 2. 50

GOGS-WOUNS (by), by God's wounds—a common oath; 3. 2. 158

GROUND, basis, (here) the lowest note; 3. 1. 73

HAGGARD, a wild hawk; 4. 1. 183

HALF-CHECKED, the checks or cheeks of a bit are the long side-pieces to which the bridle is fastened; a half-checked bit, therefore, is one with the bridle attached half-way up the cheek, thus giving inadequate leverage (cf. *Sh.Eng.* ii. 421); 3. 2. 55–6

HAND (at any), in any case; 1. 2. 144, 223

HAPPILY, haply (the words were interchangeable); 4. 4. 54

HAPPY MAN BE HIS DOLE! Proverbial = may his dole (i.e. lot) be that of a happy man; 1. 1. 138

HEAD-STALL, the part of the bridle which surrounds the head of the horse; 3. 2. 56

HEARKEN, lie in wait; 1. 2. 256

HIGH-CROSS, the cross in the centre of a town; 1. 1. 131

HILDING, jade, baggage, good-for-nothing; 2. 1. 26

HIPPED, lamed in the hip; 3. 2. 49

HOLIDAME (by my), i.e. by my Holy Dame, or by Our Lady; 5. 2. 99

HURLY, tumult; 4. 1. 193

HUSBAND (sb), housekeeper; 5. 1. 65; (vb), manage economically; Ind. i. 67

HUSHT, a variant of 'hush,' 'whist,' 'hist,' meaning 'not a word!' 1. 1. 68

INDIFFERENT, (i) impartial, not favouring either side; 1. 2. 178; (ii) ordinary, usual, correct; 4. 1. 84

INFUSED WITH, inspired with; Ind. ii. 16

INTEND, pretend; 4. 1. 193

IWIS, certainly; 1. 1. 62

JACK, (*a*) serving-man, (*b*) leather drinking-vessel; 4. 1. 46

JADE, a vicious horse. Shakespeare nearly always used it for a horse that soon tires (of either sex); 1. 2. 245; 2. 1. 201

JEALOUS, suspicious; 4. 5. 76

JILL (*a*) servant-maid, (*b*) gill, a metal drinking-vessel holding ¼ of a pint; 4. 1. 46

JOINT-STOOL, a wooden stool (made by a joiner). 'Frequently mentioned in 16th–18th c. in allusive or proverbial phrases expressing disparagement or ridicule, of which the precise explanation is lost' (N.E.D.); 2. 1. 198.

JOLLY, arrogant, overbearing; 3. 2. 211

KENNEL, gutter (channel); 4. 3. 98

KERSEY, a coarse kind of cloth; 3. 2. 65

KINDLY, naturally, e.g. (i) 'by all means!' (as we should now say); Ind. i. 14; (ii) fittingly; Ind. i. 65

KITE, falcon; 4. 1. 185

KNACK, sweetmeat, pastry; 4. 3. 67

LAMPASS, a disease in which the roof of the horse's mouth behind the front teeth swells up so as to hinder mastication; 3. 2. 51

LEAD APES IN HELL, the fate of old maids, since they could not lead children into heaven (cf. *Ado*, 2. 1. 37); 2. 1. 34

LECTURE, lesson; 3. 1. 23

LEDA'S DAUGHTER, Helen of Troy; 1. 2. 240

LEET, a court held by the lord of the manor. 'It was the predecessor of the modern police court, and like it could present for trial or indict for all crimes, and could summarily punish trivial ones' (*Sh.Eng.* i. 387); Ind. ii. 87

LEWD, vile, worthless; 4. 3. 65

LIGHT, (*a*) slightly built, (*b*) active, nimble; 2. 1. 203–4

LINK, torch, the material of burnt torches used as blacking; 4. 1. 123

LIST, strip of cloth; 3. 2. 66

LONGLY, for a long while; 1. 1. 164

LOVE IN IDLENESS, v. note; 1. 1. 150

LURE, a kind of leather frame, decked with feathers and garnished with pieces of meat, which the falconer carried in his hand; 4. 1. 182

MAN (a hawk), to accustom the bird to the presence of men, to tame; 4. 1. 183

MASQUING-STUFF, cheap material fit only for masques, or as we should now say, amateur theatricals; 4. 3. 87

MEACOCK, tame, timid, milksop; 2. 1. 306

MEAN, moderate, mild (v. note); 5. 2. 32

MERCATANTÈ, It. for 'merchant'; 4. 2. 63

MERE, absolute; Ind. i. 22

MESS, dish (cf. *L.L.L.* G.); 4. 4. 70

MI PERDONATO, pardon me; 1. 1. 25

MODESTY, self-restraint, moderation; Ind. i. 67, 93

MONUMENT, portent; 3. 2. 93

MOSE IN THE CHINE, suffer from glanders (v. note); 3. 2. 50

MUSCADEL, a sweet wine, commonly drunk by the bridal party at the conclusion of a wedding; 3. 2. 170

NAIL, 'a measure of length for cloth: 2¼ inches, or the sixteenth part of a yard' (N.E.D.); 4. 3. 109

NAIL (blow one's), an expression denoting waiting with nothing to do; we should now say 'twiddle one's thumbs' (cf. *L.L.L.* G.); 1. 1. 108

NEAR-LEGGED BEFORE, i.e. standing with the forelegs close together and the back legs wide apart (v. note); 3. 2. 55

NICE, fastidious; 3. 1. 79

NIT, the egg of a louse; 4. 3. 110

OUT-VIE, v. *vie*; 2. 1. 378

PACKING, conspiracy, plot; 5. 1. 114

PAIL (to the), 'milch-kine to the pail,' i.e. cows whose milk is not going to their calves; 2. 1. 350

PANTALOON, dotard, old fool. Orig. 'the Venetian character in Italian comedy represented as a lean and foolish old man, wearing spectacles, pantaloons and slippers' (N.E.D.); 1. 1. 47 S.D.; 3. 1. 36

PARLE, negotiation; 1. 1. 115

PASS, settle (business), settle upon; 4. 2. 118; 4. 4. 45, 57

PASSION, any powerful feeling whether of mirth or sorrow; Ind. i. 96

PAUCAS PALLABRIS, Sly's form of the Spanish 'pocas palabras' = few words (v. note and cf. *Ado*, 3. 5. 15 'palabras'); Ind. i. 5

PEAT, spoilt child, pet; 1. 1. 78

PEDASCULE, a word coined from 'pedant' on the analogy of *διδάσκαλος* (i.e. master); 3. 1. 50

PEER, to be seen peeping through; 4. 3. 172

PILLORY, a kind of stocks for the head and arms in which the culprit stood with his face framed, as it were, in wood; 2. 1. 156

PINCH, to reduce to straits (in argument), to 'put into a tight place' (N.E.D.); 2. 1. 364

PIP, 'a pip out,' v. *two and thirty*; 1. 2. 33

PITTANCE, scanty meal. The orig. meaning was a sum of money left to a religious house to provide an additional allowance of food, wine, etc. at a particular festival or anniversary; 4. 4. 61

PLACE WHERE (in), in a fit place, in the right spot; 4. 3 147–8

PLASH, pool; 1. 1. 23

PLEASANT, merry; 3. 1. 57

POINTS, the laces attaching the hose to the doublet (performing the office of buttons in modern dress); 3. 2. 48

PORT, state, style; 1. 1. 202; 3. 1. 35
PRICK, pin; 3. 2. 67
PROOF (to the), i.e. so armed as to be invulnerable; 2. 1. 140

QUAINT, cunning; 3. 2. 145; 4. 3. 102
QUALIFIED, possessed of qualities; 4. 5. 66
QUANTITY, fragment; 4. 3. 112

RANGE, (*a*) fly wide—of a falcon, (*b*) prove inconstant—of a wife; 3. 1. 91
RAYED, soiled, befouled; 3. 2. 52; 4. 1. 3
REDIME TE CAPTUM QUAM QUEAS MINIMO, free yourself from captivity at the lowest ransom you may (v. note); 1. 1. 161
RESTRAIN, draw tight; 3. 2. 57
ROPE-TRICKS, v. note; 1. 2. 111
ROUNDLY, plainly, outspokenly; 1. 2. 58; 5. 2. 21
RUDESBY, boisterous unmannerly fellow. The suffix *-by* often used in 16th and 17th c. in coining descriptive personal appellations, playful or derisive (N.E.D. '-by' 2); 3. 2. 10

SACK, white wine from Spain or the Canaries; Ind. ii. 2, 6
SADNESS, seriousness; 5. 2. 63
SENSIBLE, (*a*) something that can be felt, (*b*) striking, effective; 4. 1. 59
SESSA! Meaning doubtful. N.E.D. suggests 'sa-sa,' a common exclamation used to excite or encourage someone; formerly a cry of triumph at a hit in fencing (cf. *Lear*, 3. 4. 104; 3. 6. 77); Ind. i. 5
SHARP, famished (cf. *V.A.* 55 'an empty eagle, sharp by fast'); 4. 1. 180
SHEER ALE. Meaning doubtful, either (i) thin or small ale (cf. N.E.D. 'sheer' 5 and references to 'small ale,' Ind. ii. 1, 75), or (ii) undiluted ale (cf. N.E.D. 'sheer' 7); Ind. ii. 23
SHOULDER-SHOTTEN, with a dislocated shoulder; 3. 2. 55
SIBYL, the Sibyl of Cumae to whom Apollo granted as many years as there were grains in a handful of sand (cf. *M.V.* 1. 2. 101); 1. 2. 69
SKIPPER, light-brained, skipping fellow (cf. 1 *Hen. IV*, 3. 2. 60 'the skipping king'); 2. 1. 332
SOLEMN, ceremonial (in the sense of 'grave' rare with Shakespeare); 3. 2. 99
SPAVINS, swellings of the joints in horses; 3. 2. 52
SPECIALTY, deed, 'a special contract, obligation, or bond, expressed in an instrument under seal' (N.E.D.); 2. 1. 126
SPED, finished, done for; 3. 2. 52; 5. 2. 185
SPLEEN, sudden humour or impulse, fit of laughter or passion. Onions quotes Holland's *Pliny* 'intemperate laughers have alwaies great splenes'; Ind. i. 136; 3. 2. 10
STAGGERS, a disease in horses accompanied by giddiness; 3. 2. 53
STALE, (i) 1. 1. 58, (*a*) laughing-stock, (*b*) harlot;
(ii) 3. 1. 90, (*a*) decoy, lure (q.v.), (*b*) common fellow
STARE, swagger, behave in an overbearing manner (cf. *M.W.W.* G.); 3. 2. 226

STOCK, stocking; 3. 2. 64

STOOP. A term of falconry, meaning 'to fly to the lure' (q.v.); 4. 1. 181

STRANGE, distant, unfriendly, (here perhaps) severe (cf. *Rom.* 2. 2. 102); 1. 1. 85

SUITS (in all), in all respects (with a quibble upon 'suit' = dress); Ind. i. 105

SUPPOSES, suppositions; 5. 1. 113

SWAYED IN THE BACK, with a sunken back-bone; 3. 2. 54

SWEETING, lit. a sweet kind of apple—an appropriate term of endearment for a shrew! 4. 3. 36

SWINGE, beat, thrash; 5. 2. 104

TALL, sturdy; 4. 4. 17

TENT, bed-tester or canopy; 2. 1. 345

THIRDBOROUGH, petty constable. The word is probably a M.E. corruption of frithborough; Ind. i. 10–11

TIGHT, water-tight, sound (cf. *Temp.* 5. 1. 225); 2. 1. 372

TIME (in good), an interjection with various shades of meaning used to express acquiescence, astonishment, or indignation; 2. 1. 195

TIME (to the), to eternity, for ever; 4. 3. 97

TROT, hag; 1. 2. 78

TRUNK SLEEVE, a large wide sleeve; 4. 3. 139

TUNE (in), in a good temper (with a quibble on the more usual meaning); 3. 1. 24

TURTLE, turtle-dove, symbolical of fidelity in love; 2. 1. 207, 208

TWO AND THIRTY, A PIP OUT, not quite up to the mark. A jesting allusion, common at the period, to the game of cards called 'one-and-thirty'; 1. 2. 32–3

UNCASE, undress; 1. 1. 206

UNPINKED. To pink leather was to ornament it by scalloping and punching out a pattern upon it; 4. 1. 122

UNTOWARD, unmannerly; 4. 5. 79

USURP, assume; Ind. i. 130

VAIL, lower; 5. 2. 176

VALANCE, drapery hanging round the frame of a bedstead; 2. 1. 347

VERY (the), the mere; 4. 3. 32

VIE, (i) 'to increase in number by addition or repetition' (N.E.D.), (ii) 'in card-playing: to hazard a certain sum on the strength of one's hand' (N.E.D.); cf. *out-vie*; 2. 1. 302

WATCH, to keep a hawk awake (cf. *Oth.* 3. 3. 23 'I'll watch him tame'); 4. 1. 185

WELL SEEN, well taught; 1. 2. 132

WHITE, i.e. the white circle at the centre of the target round the pin; 5. 2. 186.

WIDOWHOOD, estate settled upon a widow (cf. *Meas.* 5. 1. 420); 2. 1. 124

WINDGALLS, a disease of the fetlock in horses; 3. 2. 52

WISH, commend; 1. 1. 112; 1. 2. 59, 63

WOODCOCK, the easiest bird to catch in a snare, and therefore a type of stupidity; 1. 2. 158

YELLOWS, the jaundice in horses; 3. 2. 52

YOUNG, strong (cf. *Ado*, 5. 1. 118); 2. 1. 232